Effects of Early Parent Death

A Volume in MSS' Series on Attitudes Toward Death

Papers by
J. Birtchnell, Ian C. Wilson, Ole Bratfos et al.

MSS Information Corporation
655 Madison Avenue, New York, N.Y. 10021

Library of Congress Cataloging in Publication Data
Main entry under title:

Effects of early parent death.

    (Attitudes toward death, v. 1)
    A collection of articles previously published in
various journals.
    1. Children and death--Addresses, essays,
lectures. 2. Parental deprivation--Addresses,
essays, lectures. I. Birtchnell, J. II. Wilson,
Ian C. III. Jacobson, Gary. IV. Series.
BF723.D3E43   155.9'37   73-10370
ISBN 0-8422-7145-7

TABLE OF CONTENTS

34234

CREDITS AND ACKNOWLEDGEMENTS

Birtchnell, J., "Early Parent Death and Psychiatric Diagnosis," *Social Psychiatry*, 1972, 7:202-210.

Birtchnell, J., "Early Parent Death in Relation to Size and Constitution of Sibship, in Psychiatric Patients and General Population Controls," *Acta Psychiatrica Scandinavica*, 1971, 47:250-270.

Birtchnell, John, "Early Parent Death and Mental Illness," *British Journal of Psychiatry*, 1970, 116:281-288.

Birtchnell, John, "Recent Parent Death and Mental Illness," *British Journal of Psychiatry*, 1970, 116:289-297.

Birtchnell, John, "The Interrelationship between Social Class, Early Parent Death, and Mental Illness," *Psychological Medicine*, 1972, 2:166-175.

Birtchnell, John, "The Possible Consequences of Early Parent Death," *British Journal of Medical Psychology*, 1969, 42:1-12.

Bratfos, Ole, "Parental Deprivation in Childhood and Type of Future Mental Disease," *Acta Psychiatrica Scandinavica*, 1967, 43:453-461.

Harrison, Saul I.; Charles W. Davenport; and John F. McDermott, Jr., "Children's Reactions to Bereavement: Adult Confusions and Misperceptions," *Archives of General Psychiatry*, 1967, 17:593-597.

Jacobson, Gary; and Robert G. Ryder, "Parental Loss and Some Characteristics of the Early Marriage Relationship," *American Journal of Orthopsychiatry*, 1969, 39:779-787.

Wilson, Ian C.; Lacoe B. Alltop; and W.J. Buffaloe, "Parental Bereavement in Childhood: M.M.P.I. Profiles in a Depressed Population," *British Journal of Psychiatry*, 1967, 113:761-764.

PREFACE

For over three decades researchers and clinicians have explored the possible relationships between early bereavement and adult mental illness. As the studies in this collection show, certain clinical groups are affected by early parent death more than others. The age of the child when he experiences his loss, his response to it, and his environment are also highly significants examined in *Effects of Early Parent Death.*

First in a new series, this volume considers diagnostic groups particularly vulnerable to pathology resulting from early bereavement. Socio-economic factors affecting early parent loss and subsequent mental illness in differing social classes are also discussed as are the effects of size and constitution of sibship in relation to early parent death. Other studies focus on parental deprivation and future mental illness, parental loss and its consequence on later marriage relationships, and children's responses to bereavement.

Effects of Early Parent Death

Early Parent Death and Psychiatric Diagnosis

J. Birtchnell

For thirty five years researchers have explored
the possible association between early bereavement
and adult mental illness. The results of the now
considerable number of studies are confusing and
part of this confusion may be due to the fact that
early bereavement affects certain clinical groups
more than others. The present study sets out to
compare the incidence of early bereavement in a
number of diagnostic groups and a general population sample in order to determine whether in fact
such groups are affected differentially. In making
such comparisons it is important to remember that
the incidence of early bereavement varies with decade of birth (Fig. 1) and also that there is a significant variation in the decade of birth distribution
for different diagnostic groups (Table 1). In the present study the incidence of early bereavement in
each diagnostic group will be compared with that of
a hypothetical group of the general population, of
similar decade of birth distribution, calculated from
the general population sample. Though the incidence
of early bereavement also varies with parental social class (Birtchnell, 1971) there is no significant
variation in the parental social class distribution of
different diagnostic groups (Birtchnell, 1970c). This
factor can therefore be safely ignored in the present
study.

11

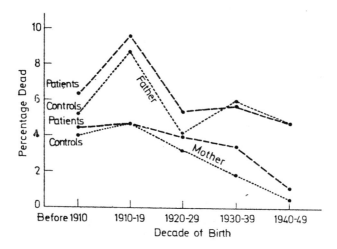

Fig. 1. The Incidence of parent death occurring before age ten by year of birth in psychiatric patients and general population controls.

There have been a number of studies of this type carried out in America. The first was that of Oltman McGarry and Friedman (1952) in Newtown, Connecticut in which six diagnostic groups were compared with a small sample of 230 mental hospital employees. The data of this study were subjected to more detailed analysis by Gregory (1958), who pointed out that it is doubtful whether hospital employees can be considered representative of the general population, because of their personality and sociocultural characteristics, and also that the mean age of this control group was probably appreciably higher than that of some of the patient groups. There was no attempt to match for age, and the incidence of parental death occurring before age 19 did not differ from that in the control group for any of the diagnostic groups. Oltman and Friedman subsequently published a series of studies (1965, 1966 and 1967) from the same location with larger numbers of patients in a variety of diagnostic groups and with a larger control sample (350). These controls were again mental hospital employees and it was stated that they represented only 45 per cent of subjects written to. This can hardly be accepted as a reliable sample. Bereavement data were presented by decade of birth and, though the authors did not do so, it is possible to calculate age - rèlated expected numbers of bereaved patients, for each diagnostic group, from the control sample. When this is done it would

12

appear that significantly more than expected of the schizophrenics, alcoholics and psychoneurotics were bereaved of their fathers before age 19. On the other hand significantly fewer than expected of the schizophrenics, alcoholics and affective disorders were bereaved of their mothers by the same age. These findings are unusual and are probably due to the fact that the control sample was too small to reliably calculate age-related expected numbers. In 1959 Gregory conducted a study of 1 000 consecutive admissions to an Ontario hospital. For comparison he calculated the incidence of mothers and fathers, aged 30 and 35 respectively at the birth of the child, who would be dead when the child was aged 5, 10, 15 and 20, from age, sex specific death rates for the province of Ontario, 1921-51. He was not able to take into account the difference in age-structure of the various diagnostic groups. He concluded that death of a father before the age of ten years exceeded the expected frequency in the youngest schizophrenic group, in manic depressive psychoses and the psychoneuroses; and death of a mother during the same period exceeded the expected frequency in all schizophrenic age groups. None of these excesses were statistically significant. In 1962 he published a report of the incidence of early bereavement in 370 admissions to Minnesota hospitals. In this study he presented no control data and only compared the incidence of early bereavement between various diagnostic groups. By 1966 he had extended this series to include 980 cases; however, as he used eight diagnoses, the numbers in each group were still relatively small. Furthermore he was not able to examine early bereavement separately, in relation to decade of birth, but only all types of loss grouped together. In neither of these Minnesota studies did significant findings emerge. In 1965, Pitts, Meyer, Brooks and Winokur carried out a carefully planned study of 748 consecutive admissions to the psychiatric division of a large general hospital in St. Louis, Missouri. They compared these with 250 consecutive admissions to the obstetrical, medical and surgical wards of the same hospital, who matched the psychiatric patients by age sex and whether or not they were private. When comparisons were made between the six diagnostic groups and the control sample, sub groups matched by age sex and hospital status were extracted for each diagnostic group. The numbers were small for the detailed comparisons which were carried out but no significant differences in the incidence of early bereavement were shown to exist between patients

13

and controls, regardless of the age at death of parent. In 1966, Brill and Liston compared the incidence of early bereavement in 5479 patients referred to the psychiatric service of a neuropsychiatric institute in Los Angeles with estimates of early bereavement in the United States population obtained from the Metropolitan Life Insurance company statistical reports and a mental health survey of the United States carried out by Gurin et al. (1960, 1966). Such comparisons did not of course allow for regional variations in death rates which undoubtedly exist. No mention was made of adjustment for decade of birth either in the total patient group or in comparisons with separate diagnostic groups. No significant differences emerged from the study.

In Scandinavia two studies of this type have been reported. In 1967 Bratfos surveyed the case records of 4 000 patients admitted to the Psychiatric Department of the University of Oslo, Norway. No control group was used and no adjustment was made for decade of birth. The incidence of parent death occurring before age 15 was shown not to differ significantly between four diagnostic groups. In 1968 Kettner published a preliminary report of a more carefully executed study carried out in the University Department of Psychiatry, Uppsala, Sweden on a series of 997 patients. Each was matched with a control subject of the same sex, born next after him in the same parish. The dates of the parents' birth and death were also obtained from the parish records. The neurotics and sociopaths combined lost their mothers before age 10 significantly more often than their controls. The manic depressives lost their fathers before age 15 significantly more often than their controls. These relationships were most marked for women patients. (Some of this information was obtained by personal communication.)

Finally there have been two British studies of this type reported. Dennehy in 1966 personally interviewed 1020 patients in three mental hospitals serving areas of central London. She had no control group but calculated the probability of losing a parent before age 15 by year of birth from graphs constructed from data obtained from the 1921 Census, the Chester Beattie Serial Abridged Life Tables (1962) and for fathers, the numbers of women receiving widows' Pensions (1959). For more detailed analysis by age at death of parent she made direct comparisons with 1921 Census data, with no adjustment for decade of birth. These latter findings were therefore less reliable. She found that death of mother before age 15

Table 1. Percentage distribution by decade of birth and sex in five diagnostic groups. Expected numbers were derived from the total distributions.

		Before 1900	1900 -09	1910 -19	1920 -29	1930 -39	1940 -49	Total	$\frac{(O-E)^2}{E}$	P (d.f. = 5)
Depression	Men	11.1	23.2	20.1	21.9	15.2	8.4	775	130.4790	<.001
	Women	11.9	16.5	18.3	23.0	19.5	10.7	1924	57.8027	<.001
Neurosis other than depression	Men	1.4	8.8	14.1	32.6	27.9	15.2	362	30.7436	<.001
	Women	3.1	4.9	12.1	24.7	38.2	16.9	489	101.01	<.001
Psychosis other than depressive	Men	6.0	8.7	13.3	33.6	26.6	11.9	369	18.6419	<.005
	Women	10.7	12.4	22.9	29.9	18.7	5.5	402	35.9388	<.001
Alcoholism	Men	4.6	13.2	25.5	31.4	21.2	4.1	439	46.1538	<.001
	Women	7.8	16.9	20.8	36.4	16.9	1.3	77	16.3646	<.01
Personality Disorder	Men	0.5	3.8	10.3	25.5	27.6	32.2	369	165.3143	<.001
	Women	2.6	3.4	11.6	17.3	35.2	29.8	352	152.1627	<.001
Total	Men	135	316	406	644	512	301	2314	-	-
	Women	302	417	561	772	775	417	3244	-	-

15

significantly exceeded the expected incidence for alcoholics, male depressives and male schizophrenics and that death of father before age 15 did so for depressives, male schizophrenics, male alcoholics and male drug addicts. Munro and Griffiths (1969) conducted a such smaller study of 279 psychiatric patients treated in and around Leeds and a control group of 100 general hospital out-patients. They made no adjustment for decade of birth. Apart from a just significant excess of maternal bereavement before age 15 in in-patient depressives, which was probably related to age, they found no significant differences between the three diagnostic groups examined.

The present study has advantages over those reported upon in this review in that a large patient sample is used, providing substantial numbers in the major diagnostic categories, the control sample is of adequate size and is derived from the local population, separate comparisons are made in respect of the relatively early age period of 0-9, which has been previously shown to be the period during which early bereavement is most likely to be significantly related to adult mental illness (Birtchnell 1970 and 1971) and all expected numbers are based upon the decade of birth distribution of the diagnostic groups.

Method

The source of the psychiatric patient sample was the North-Eastern Regional Psychiatric Case Register (Scotland) which has been in operation in the Department of Mental Health of the University of Aberdeen since January 1963 (Baldwin, Innes, Millar, Sharp and Dorricott, 1965). A very high proportion of patients referred to the regional psychiatric services are interviewed by trained staff who record social and family data on standard forms. The forms are stored in numerical sequence in the Mental Health Research Unit. Some of the data are coded and stored on magnetic tape files for use on the university computer. Unfortunately detailed information on early parent death is not included in the magnetic tape store. Additional codes were devised therefore and the extra data needed were extracted and coded from the original survey forms. In a substantial proportion of cases the patients' records were incomplete. To obtain these missing data a postal survey was carried out and patients who were currently in hospital were interviewed again. There remained 8.0 per cent for whom information about the death of their fathers was not precisely known. However this included 4.2 per cent who were known to be illegitimate and 1.8 per cent who were brought up in institutions or foster homes. There were only 3.1 per cent for whom information about the death of their mothers was not precisely known and this included 2.5 per cent who were brought up in institutions or foster homes.

The psychiatric sample comprised 6 795 patients aged 20 or over who were referred to the psychiatric services in the North-Eastern Region during the five year period 1963 - 7. For each patient the diagnosis was taken as the last one available in the record. If the case was closed this was the discharge diagnosis, otherwise it was that of the latest admission. Diagnosis was coded according to the International Classification of Diseases, Seventh Revision. Each diagnostic group used in the study included a predetermined set of disease classifications. Depression included 301.1, 302, 314 and 688, Neurosis other than depressive, 310 - 313 and 315 - 318, Psychosis other than depressive, 300, 301.0, 301.2 and 303, Alcoholism and drug addiction, 307, 322 and 323, and Personality disorders 320, 321, 324 and 326. Patients in other diagnostic groups (17.3 per cent of the sample) were omitted from the comparisons.

The general population sample was obtained by postal survey. A systematic random sample of 4 000 subjects aged 20 or over was selected from lists of seven general practices in the North-Eastern Region of Scotland. Questionnaires together with a covering letter were sent to these subjects, with reminder letters after appropriate intervals. Replies were received from 3 425 of them (85.6 %) and these subjects were used as the control group. They were comparable in age and sex distribution to the psychiatric sample though not precisely matched. There were only 4.5 per cent without precise information about paternal deaths. These included 1.7 per cent who were known to be illegitimate and 1.0 per cent who were brought up in institutions or foster homes. There were 1.7 per cent without precise information about maternal deaths and these included 1.1 per cent who were brought up in institutions or foster homes. These cases were excluded from the denominators in all calculations.

Parental death was in all cases that of the natural parent and not of a step-parent, foster parent or person who had come to be looked upon as a parent. As it is a study of the number of bereaved individuals and not of the number of parents who have died, when two parents had died during the period of childhood considered, only the first to die was counted; when two parents had died during the same year of childhood each was counted separately under the appropriate parent.

As there was a significant variation in the decade of birth distribution within the different diagnostic groups, it was necessary to calculate from the control sample expected incidences of early parent death, based upon this distribution for each diagnostic group separately. The expected incidence may be expressed as Σ ni when n is the number of patients in an age group and i is the incidence of early parental deaths in that age group in the general population sample.

Fig. 1 demonstrates clearly that, in North-East Scotland, during the first half of this century, the incidence of parental bereavement before age ten bore a definite relationship to decade of birth. The relationship was markedly different for paternal and maternal bereavement and it is noteworthy that, in this respect, the trends for patients and controls resembled each other closely. The incidence of paternal bereavement has been obviously influenced by the two World Wars. The sharp peak for subjects born between 1910 and 1919 was due to World War I and the lesser peak for those born between 1930 and 1939 was due to World War II. The slight rise in the incidence of maternal bereavement for subjects born between 1910 and 1919 was probably due to the influenza epidemic of 1919.

Fig. 2 shows a less clear cut relationship between the incidence of parental bereavement occurring from age ten to nineteen and decade of birth. Again the trends for patients and controls resembled each other closely. Both showed a gradual decline in the incidence of paternal and maternal bereavement throughout the first half of the century. This time the effects of the 1914-18 war would be apparent only in those born before 1910.

Table 1 shows the very marked variation in decade of birth distribution which exists among the five diagnostic groups considered in the present study. The personality disorders occur predominantly in the younger age groups; the neurotics, psychotics and alcoholics extend over a wider age range; and the depressives occur more during middle age and later life. In view of this it is surprising how little attention has been paid to adjustment for age in many previous studies.

18

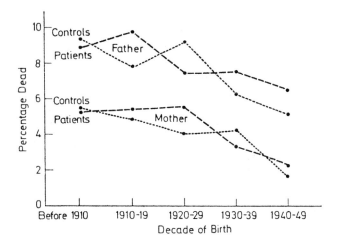

Fig. 2. The incidence of parent death occuring from age ten to nineteen in psychiatric patients and general population controls.

Table 2 shows the incidence of parent death oc- curring before age ten, in each of the five diagnostic groups, compared with what it would be expected to be in a general population group of similar decade of birth distribution. There were no significant dif- ferences between the observed and the expected in- cidence of early bereavement in the neurotic patients. In the psychotic patients there was a barely signifi- cant excess of early mother death for women only (p. < .05). In the personality disorders the only sig- nificant finding was an overall excess of early be- reavement for women (p < .025), though this was not evident when father or mother deaths were consid- ered separately. The alcoholic men showed no sig- nificant difference between the observed and the ex- pected. The small number of alcoholic women on the other hand, exceeded the expected to highly sig- nificant extent (p < .001) and early father death ap- peared to be more important than early mother death. The most striking deviations from the ex- pected occurred in depressed patients. As with the other diagnostic groups, early parent death appear- ed to be most important for the women (p < .001): there were significant excesses for both early fa- ther (p < .005) and early mother (p < .01) death. In the case of the depressed men there was only a just significant excess of early mother death (p < .05).

Table 2. The incidence of parent death occurring before the age of ten in five diagnostic groups. The expected numbers, based upon the age distribution within the diagnostic groups, were calculated from the general population sample. The incidence is expressed as a percentage of patients for whom information about the death of the parent was known

Diagnosis		Father		Mother		Either	
		Sons	Daughters	Sons	Daughters	Sons	Daughters
Depression (775 sons, 1924 daughters)	Observed	51 (7.0%)	120 (6.7%)	36 (4.8%)	80 (4.2%)	87 (11.9%)	200 (11.2%)
	Expected	47.1	92.4	25.6	58.9	72.7	151.3
	$\frac{(O-E)^2}{E}$	0.3229 N.S.	8.2442 p<.005	4.2250 p<.05	7.5587 p<.01	2.8128 N.S.	15.6754 p<.001
Neurosis other than depressive (362 sons, 489 daughters)	Observed	18 (5.3%)	25 (5.3%)	7 (2.0%)	17 (3.6%)	25 (7.5%)	42 (9.0%)
	Expected	20.1	24.3	9.4	11.8	29.5	36.1
	$\frac{(O-E)^2}{E}$	0.2194 N.S	0.0202 N.S.	0.6128 N.S.	2.2915 N.S.	0.6864 N.S.	0.9643 N.S.
Psychosis other than depressive (369 sons, 402 daughters)	Observed	16 (4.7%)	19 (5.2%)	12 (3.3%)	21 (15.4%)	28 (8.2%)	40 (10.9%)
	Expected	20.6	19.4	10.3	13.0	30.9	32.4
	$\frac{(O-E)^2}{E}$	1.0272 N.S.	0.0082 N.S.	0.2806 N.S.	4.9231 p<.05	0.2722 N.S.	1.7827 N.S.

Table 2

Diagnosis		Father		Mother		Either	
		Sons	Daughters	Sons	Daughters	Sons	Daughters
Alcoholism (439 sons, 77 daughters)	Observed	23 (5.6%)	9 (12.5%)	15 (3.5%)	6 (7.8%)	38 (9.4%)	15 (20.8%)
	Expected	26.5	3.6	14.2	2.6	40.7	6.2
	$\frac{(O-E)^2}{E}$	0.4623 N.S.	8.1000 $p<.005$	0.0451 N.S.	4.4462 $p<.05$	0.1791 N.S.	12.4903 $p<.001$
Personality disorder (369 sons, 352 daughters)	Observed	25 (7.7%)	25 (7.9%)	9 (2.5%)	11 (3.2%)	34 (10.6%)	36 (11.5%)
	Expected	17.6	17.3	7.5	7.4	25.1	24.7
	$\frac{(O-E)^2}{E}$	3.1114 N.S.	3.4272 N.S.	0.3000 N.S.	1.7514 N.S.	3.1558 N.S.	5.1696 $p<.025$

Table 3 shows the incidence of parent death occurring from age ten to nineteen in the same five
diagnostic groups, together with decade of birth
based expected incidences again derived from the
control sample. This time the observed and expected incidences in all five diagnostic groups corresponded closely and there were no significant differences.

Discussion

The present investigation was planned to make
good some of the deficiencies of an earlier study
carried out at the Crichton Royal Hospital, Dumfries which involved only 500 psychiatric admissions
and a matched control group of similar size (Birtchnell, 1969 and 1970 a and b). These numbers were
hardly adequate to accurately assess the relationship of early parent death to decade of birth (1969)
or to consider the possible variation with diagnosis
(1970a p. 281.). Considering first, the relationship
to decade of birth, the numbers of subjects in each
decade of birth group are very much larger in the
present study, so that the incidence of early bereavement by decade of birth was calculated with more
certainty. It was clearly demonstrated that, apart
from a slight rise at the time of the influenza epidemic of 1919, the incidence of mother death occurring before age ten has declined steadily in recent
decades. That of father death occurring during the
same age span has shown no such improvement.
There was a marked increase at the time of the 1914
-18 War and the 1919 epidemic and another small
increase at the time of the 1939-45 War. For those
subjects born in the decade 1940-49 it remained approximately 4 per cent higher than that of early mother death. Decade of birth must therefore be considered an important variable in early parent death studies. The correspondence between the graphs of the
patients and the controls (Fig. 1) is reassuring and
lends support to their validity. It is tempting to infer,
that those decades during which the graphs of the two
samples deviate most, represent the age periods
when the pathological effects of early bereavement
were most potent. It is unlikely however that patients
under the age of 40 were more affected by the early
death of their mothers and those older than this were
more affected by that of their fathers. The more
probable explanation is that these age groups are
more representative of the diagnostic groups most
positively related to early bereavement. The rela-

22

tionship between parental death occurring from age ten to nineteen (Fig. 2) has shown a gradual decline in recent decades.

Because in the Crichton Royal study the numbers were too small to reliably compare several diagnostic groups, by way of a compromise, the incidence of early bereavement was compared in samples of depressed and non-depressed patients, matched for age, extracted from the total patient group (1970b). No significant differences emerged; though, within the depressed group the severely ill patients had experienced significantly more early bereavement than the moderately ill ones. This was in contrast to the previously reported finding of Hill and Price (1967) that the incidence of father death before age 15 was significantly higher in 1 483 depressed patients than in 1 059 non-depressed ones, making allowance for the difference in decade of birth distribution. The Aberdeen study clearly shows that the composition of the non-depressed group would be an important variable in this type of comparison. There were, in Hill and Price's non-depressed group, at least 55 % comprising organic and neurotic patients, who, from the findings of the present study, should have experienced a normal incidence of early bereavement. There was a much smaller proportion of such cases in the Crichton Royal non-depressed group, which probably explains why the incidence of early bereavement was similar to that in the depressed group. Munro and Griffiths (1969) on the other hand, suggested that the composition of the depressed patients was the decisive factor in this type of study. They stated "It seems likely that the nearer the diagnosis is to "endogenous" or "manic-depressive" depression, the less important is parental deprivation in the actual aetiology". and "When the depressive illness is contaminated by certain extraneous psychiatric conditions, the rate of deprivation may be found to be high, but this is not necessarily related to the depression itself". Because such conditions as psychopathy and delinquency have been reported to be associated with "severe childhood disturbances" Munro and Griffiths believed that the inclusion of such patients in a sample of depressives would increase the incidence of parental deprivation. There are two important faults in their argument: (i) the type of disturbed home background associated with psychopathy and delinquency should not be likened to early parent death; and (ii) the majority of studies have not reported a high incidence of early parent death among psychopaths and delinquents. In the

23

Table 3. The incidence of parent death occurring from age ten to nineteen in five diagnostic groups. The expected numbers, based upon the age distribution within the diagnostic groups, were calculated from the general population sample.

Diagnosis		Father Sons	Father Daughters	Mother Sons	Mother Daughters	Either Sons	Either Daughters
Depression (775 sons, 1924 daughters)	Observed	60	158	41	84	101	242
	Expected	52.5	150.6	35.4	75.1	87.9	225.7
	$\frac{(O-E)^2}{E}$	1.0714 N.S.	0.3612 N.S.	0.8859 N.S.	1.0547 N.S.	1.9523 N.S.	1.1772 N.S.
Neurosis other than depressive (362 sons, 489 daughters)	Observed	24	36	13	12	37	48
	Expected	22.3	36.8	15.8	16.9	38.1	53.7
	$\frac{(O-E)^2}{E}$	0.1296 N.S.	0.0174 N.S.	0.4962 N.S.	1.4207 N.S.	0.0318 N.S.	0.6050 N.S.

Table 3

Diagnosis		Father		Mother		Either	
		Sons	Daughters	Sons	Daughters	Sons	Daughters
Psychosis other than depressive (369 sons, 402 daughters)	Observed	28	29	20	25	48	54
	Expected	22.5	31.9	16.4	15.6	49.9	47.5
	$\frac{(O-E)^2}{E}$	1.3444 N.S.	0.2636 N.S.	0.7902 N.S.	5.6641 p<.02	0.0723 N.S.	0.8895 N.S.
Alcoholism (439 sons, 77 daughters)	Observed	24	8	19	4	43	12
	Expected	28.2	6.6	20.3	3.2	48.5	9.8
	$\frac{(O-E)^2}{E}$	0.6255 N.S.	0.2970 N.S.	0.0833 N.S.	0.2000 N.S.	0.6237 N.S.	0.4939 N.S.
Personality disorder (369 sons, 352 daughters)	Observed	23	24	10	7	33	31
	Expected	19.7	24.0	14.3	11.1	34.0	35.1
	$\frac{(O-E)^2}{E}$	0.5528 N.S.	0.0000 N.S.	1.2930 N.S.	1.5144 N.S.	0.0294 N.S.	0.4798 N.S.

present study, for example, the incidence of early bereavement in the personality disorders was no higher than that in the depressives. In fact, in a paper published in the same year, Munro (1969), clearly demonstrated that as the diagnosis of depression was refined there was a gradual tendency for the incidence of early parent death to be increased.

The advantage of the present (Aberdeen) study is that the patient and control samples were comparatively large. This made it possible to consider five diagnostic groups separately and, within each group, to calculated precisely decade of birth-adjusted expected numbers of early bereaved patients. The study confirmed the finding of the previous (Dumfries) one (Birtchnell 1970a) that the critical period for parental bereavement is before the age of ten. In the main, the observed incidence of parent death occurring from age ten to nineteen corresponded closely with what would be expected on the basis of the decade of birth distribution. Again, in agreement with the Dumfries study, it would appear that women are more affected by early parent death than are men. Apart from the suggestion that early mother death may be important for male depressives, there were no significant findings for male patients considered separately. The study showed that early parent death is not a factor in neurosis or, with the possible exception of early mother death for women, in psychosis. The women patients for whom the association with early bereavement was strongest were the depressives and the alcoholics. There appeared to be a less marked association with the personality disorders. The sex of the parent lost did not seem to matter, for in those diagnoses when there was a significant excess of early bereavement, the excess was for both early mothers and early father death.

It is perhaps reassuring that the adult illness most positively associated with early bereavement is depression, for previous writers (Brown 1961, Bowlby 1961) have proposed that adult depressive illness may in some respects be a re-enactment of childhood grief, or even a release of pent-up, unexpressed grief from this earlier period. This explanation is not entirely acceptable, for adult depression is different in a number of respects from the state of grief. It may be, however, that the early loss of a parent may create in the individual a general sense of insecurity, such that he is particularly vulnerable to isolation or rejection in adult life. Barry, Barry and Lindemann (1965) claimed to have shown that early bereaved patients, compared with later bereaved ones, demonstrated a dependent clinging type of personality and demanded a great deal of time and attention from their doctors. They added "Depression is not a surprising finding in such a group, because dependency needs are not likely to be satisfied if they are excessive, and inability to fulfill or gratify them might easily result in fanciful or real rejection". It is probable too, of course, that such individuals may sometimes succumb to alcoholism.

The fact that only women appear to be affected by early bereavement is less easy to explain. It could be argued that women are compelled to be dependent upon men by virtue of their domestic and maternal responsibilities and tend to lead a more isolated existence when their husbands are away at their work. In a recent study of attempted suicide 54.7% of the women admitted to feeling lonely and unwanted (Birtchnell and Alarcon, 1971).

It is disquieting that the results of the present study differ in several respects from those of the other British comparative study carried out by Dennehy (1966) in the London area. She observed in male alcoholics and male schizophrenics a significant excess of both mother and father death before age 15. In the present study there were no positive findings for male alcoholics or for schizophrenics of either sex. In the depressives she observed a significant excess of early father death for men which was not confirmed by the present study, but no significant excess of early mother death for women, which was shown in the present study. The two studies were in agreement in respect of the other findings for depressives.

Acknowledgements. The study forms part of a larger investigation of familial factors in mental illness involving the North Eastern Regional Psychiatric Case Register and a local population control group. During the early part of the study the author held a Medical Research Council Clinical Research Fellowship. I am indebted to Dr. John Baldwin for his assistance in planning and carrying out the project and to Mr. John Evans for organising the Aberdeen computer search. Dr. C.C. Spicer, Director of the M.R.C. Computer Unit, London, devised a programme for the analysis of the data and the analyses were carried out by Miss Valerie Coulson. I am most grateful to Professor Ian Richardson, Director of the General Practice Teaching and Research Unit, Aberdeen, and the General Practitioners of the North-Eastern Region of Scotland for their generous cooperation in the general population survey. I should also like to thank the technical and clerical staff of the Mental Health Research Unit, Aberdeen, and a number of temporary research assistants, who were paid by a supplementary grant from the M.R.C., for their help in the tedious collection and preparation of the data. Finally I should like to express my appreciation of the encouragement and advice of Dr. Peter Sainsbury and other members of the M.R.C. Clinical Psychiatry Unit in Chichester.

References

Baldwin, J.A., Innes, G., Millar, W.M., Sharp, G.A., Dorricott, N.: A psychiatric case register in North-Eastern Scotland. Brit. J. Prev. Soc. Med. 19, 38-42 (1965).

Barry, H. Jr., Barry, H. III, Lindemann, E.: Dependency in adult patients following early maternal bereavement. J. Nerv. Mental Dis. 140, 196-206 (1965).

Birtchnell, J.: Parent death in relation to age and parental age at birth in psychiatric patients and general population controls. Brit. J. Prev. Soc. Med. 23, 244-250 (1969).

Birtchnell, J.: Early parent death and mental illness. British J. Psychiat. 116, 281-288 (1970a).

Birtchnell, J.: Depression in relation to early and recent parent death. Brit. J. Psychiat. 116, 299-306 (1970b).

Birtchnell, J.: Sibship Size and Mental Illness, Brit. J. Psychiat. 117, 303-308 (1970c).

Birtchnell, J.: A case register study of bereavement. Proc. Royal Soc. Med. 64, 279-282 (1971).

Birtchnell, J., Alarcon, J.: The motivation and emotional state of 91 cases of attempted suicide. Brit. J. Med. Psychol. 44, 45-52 (1971).

Bowlby, J.: The Adolf Meyer Lecture. Childhood mourning and its implications for psychiatry. Amer. J. Psychiat. 118, 481-498 (1961).

Bratfos, O.: Parental deprivation in childhood and type of future mental disease. Acta psychiat. Scand. 43, 453-461 (1967).

Brill, N.O., Liston, E.H.: Parental loss in adults with emotional disorders. Arch. Gen. Psychiat. 14, 307-314 (1966).

Brown, F.: Depression and childhood bereavement. J. ment. Sci. 107, 754-777 (1961).

Dennehy, C. M.: Childhood bereavement and psychiatric illness. Brit. J. Psychiat. 112, 1049-1069 (1966).

Gregory, J.: Studies of parental deprivation in psychiatric patients. Amer. J. Psychiat. 115, 432-442 (1958).

Gregory, I.: An analysis of family data on 1 000 patients admitted to a Canadian mental hospital, Acta Genet. 9, 54-96 (1959).

Gregory, I.: Selected personal and familial data on 400 psychiatric inpatients. Amer. J. Psychiat. 119, 397-403 (1962).

Gregory, I.: Retrospective data concerning childhood loss of a parent. Il Category of parental loss by decade of birth, diagnosis and MMPI. Arch. Gen. Psychiat. 15, 362-367 (1966).

Gurin, G., Veroff, J., Feld, S.: Americans View of their Mental Health. New York: Basic Books, Inc. 1960.

Gurin, G., Veroff, J. Feld, S.: Tabular Supplement to Americans' View of their Mental Health. Ann Arbor, Mich.: Survey Research Centre. 1966.

Hill, O. W., Price, J. S.: Childhood bereavement and adult depression. Brit. J. Psychiat. 113, 743-751 (1967).

Kettner, B.: Early parental loss and mental illness. Acta psychiat. scand., Suppl. 203, 81-83 (1968).

Kettner, B.: Personal communication. 1970.

Munro, A.: How to make parental deprivation seem important in depressive illness. Int. Mental Health Res. Newsl. 11, 10-14 (1969).

Munro, A., Griffiths, A. B.: Some psychiatric non-sequelae of childhood bereavement. Brit. J. Psychiat. 115, 305-311 (1969).

Oltman, J. E., Friedman, S.: Report on parental deprivation in psychiatric disorders. I In Schizophrenia. Arch. Gen. Psychiat. 12, 46-57 (1965).

Oltman, J. E., Friedman, S.: Parental deprivation in psychiatric disorders. II In affective Illnesses. Dis. nerv. Syst. 27, 239-244 (1966).

Oltman, J. E., Friedman, S.: Parental deprivation in psychiatric conditions. III In personality disorders and other conditions. Dis. nerv. Syst. 28, 298-303 (1967).

Oltman, J. E., McGarry, J. J., Friedman, S.: Parental deprivation and the "broken home" in dementia praecox and other mental disorders. Amer. J. Psychiat. 108, 685-694 (1952).

Pitts, F. N. Jr., Meyer, J., Brooks, M., Winokur, G.: Adult psychiatric illness assessed for childhood parental loss and psychiatric illness in family members - a study of 748 patients and 250 controls. Amer. J. Psychiat. 121, Supplement 12, i-x. (1965).

The possible consequences of early parent death

By JOHN BIRTCHNELL

The possible effects of early parent death have been considered by a variety of investigators, each with a different emphasis and from a different theoretical standpoint. Epidemiologists have attempted to demonstrate a raised incidence of parent death in childhood in psychiatric patients compared with general population estimates or matched control groups. Child psychiatrists have observed the reactions of children and other family members to the death of a parent and have predicted that such an event might have serious long-term consequences. Analysts have been convinced that the symptoms of certain patients have been related to the incomplete mourning of a parent who died during the patient's childhood. Sociologists have suggested that the absence of a parent for long periods might result in serious disturbance of family function and of individual development. Finally, Munro (1965) has stressed that children experience parental bereavement much more commonly than is generally realized and many would appear to make a satisfactory adjustment to the loss. The intention of the present paper is to coordinate the theories of various investigators and to present a comprehensive picture of the suggested possible consequences of death of a parent occurring in childhood.

Parent death and subsequent delinquency or criminal behaviour

From the early 1930s there was a growing conviction that separation of an infant from its mother resulted in severe disturbance of personality. Levy (1937) described an 8-year-old girl who, after she had been adopted, was brought to him because of her stealing. She had been cared for by a succession of foster mothers and her characteristic features were the superficiality of her social relationships, her incapacity to form attachments and her lack of emotional responsiveness. He claimed to have found frequent evidence of 'primary affect hunger' in the children brought to him for treatment. Bowlby (1946), in a study of 44 juvenile thieves, found 14 to be affection-less, and of these 12 had suffered early or prolonged separation from their mothers or mother-figures during the first 5 years of life. Of the remaining 30 thieves only five had suffered similar separation. Bowlby (1951, p. 34) proposed that 'there is a specific connexion between prolonged deprivation in the early years and the development of an affectionless psychopathic character given to persistent delinquent conduct and extremely difficult to treat .

Spitz (1945, 1946, 1949) carried out a number of studies of children admitted to hospital at an early age. He concluded that children who had been well cared for by their mothers for the first six months of life reacted to separation by becoming apathetic, silent and sad. He called this state 'anaclitic depression'. Recovery was rapid if the child was restored to its mother, but after three months of separation recovery was rarely, if ever, complete. Goldfarb (1943 a, b, 1944, 1947) studied children admitted to a very harsh institution during the first few months of life and retained until they were 3 years old. He too found a high proportion to be detached, isolated and incapable of deep or lasting ties. Follow-up studies revealed that the degree of reversal of the basic impairment was of limited degree. Burlingham & Freud (1944) observed similar reactions in a group of young concentration-camp victims who had undergone repeated traumatic separations from birth or infancy. Anna Freud (1960) has subsequently reported that these children, though apparently stable during the latency period, became withdrawn, moody and hostile from pre-adolescence onwards.

It is generally agreed that for the first three months of life the infant is intimately bound to its mother in an undifferentiated manner. This is called infantile narcissism by Anna Freud and the phase of normal autism by Mahler (1961). From 4 to 6 months onwards the infant becomes partially separated and is able to perceive the mother as an object for libidinal cathexis. At about the same time she becomes an internalized object with which the infant may relate. When the state of object constancy is reached the mother's image may be maintained internally irrespective of her presence in the real world. Mahler calls this the symbiotic phase. It is from this moment onwards that the infant is capable of appreciating the loss of the object and of attempting to regain it. Anna Freud (1960) states:

We have always considered the interval between loss of contact with the mother and attachment to the substitute mother as the period most productive of pathology, especially if this interval is prolonged either for external reasons (lack of suitable substitute mother) of for internal reasons (inability to transfer cathexis).

Bowlby (1960) has described precisely the phases of angry protest, despair and detachment which occur when a child between the age of 6 months and 3 years is separated from its mother. It is the third phase which corresponds to the descriptions of separated children noted above. Regarding replacement Bowlby remarks:

Provided there is one particular mother figure to whom he can relate he will in time take to her and treat her in some respects as though she was his mother. In those situations where the child has no single person to whom he can relate, on the other hand, or where there is a succession of persons to whom he makes brief attachments, the outcome is, of course, different. As a rule he becomes increasingly self-centred and prone to make transient and shallow relationships with all and sundry.

Though it is clear that, under certain circumstances, a relationship exists between prolonged or repeated separation from a mother and the inability to form deep and lasting relationships, it is unwise to conclude that maternal deprivation is the only factor or that it invariably has such an effect. Regarding the effects of institutionalization, Wooton (1962, p. 66) remarks:

One is, however, left with the impression that those children were not as a rule very intelligently or even always very kindly treated. Nor had sufficient weight generally been given to the possibility that communal homes for children may differ from families in other respects besides the opportunity which they offer for intimate affectionate relationships.

It is most likely that what is lacking in institutionalized children is not specifically maternal affection but a normal family life. Bowlby *et al.* (1956), comparing children in a tuberculosis sanitorium and a group of healthy children, discovered that few of the sanitorium children became delinquent. Lewis (1954), studying 500 children admitted to a reception centre, concluded that 'Neither delinquency nor incapacity for affectionate relationships was significantly more frequent in the separated children.' Andry (1955, p. 357) concluded from an examination of 80 delinquents and 80 controls that 'Separation between a child and one or other of both parents...do not seem to be primary factors in the aetiology of delinquency.' Howells (1959) has maintained that the greater number of children who are deprived of mothering are in fact living with the mother and are not separated from her. Implicit in this statement is that the type of parent rather than her presence or absence is the more important factor.

Parent death is a special kind of separation in that it is permanent, that it is not a reflexion of previous parental disharmony or mental illness and that it is a normal inevitable event. It resembles more a clean surgical incision than a dirty gash due to trauma. Even in 1934 Sutherland considered (p. 145) that 'According to the rather scanty evidence, delinquency is less likely to result from a break caused by death than from a break caused by desertion, divorce or separation.' Brown & Epps (1966) demonstrated that disorders of conduct in children were not associated with parent death but with other separation experiences. Glueck & Glueck (1950) showed that 60·4 per cent of 500 delinquent boys, compared with 34·2 per cent of 500 non-delinquent boys, came from broken homes. Homes broken by abandonment, desertion, absence due to divorce or separation occurred in 36·2 per cent of delinquent boys compared with 12·8 per cent of non-delinquent boys, whereas the figures for death of a parent were 12·4 per cent and 10·6 per cent respectively. Broken homes due to separation or divorce must be the culmination of longstanding marital disturbances. It is reasonable to conclude that delinquent behaviour is probably a reflexion of disturbed behaviour in parents and that separation is a further manifestation of this behaviour.

Parent death in relation to
mourning and depression

The syndromes of adult grief and mourning have been fully described by Lindemann (1944), Wretmark (1959) and Engel (1961). Freud (1917, p. 245) observed that 'Each single one of the memories and expectations in which the libido is bound to the object is brought up and hypercathected, and detachment of the libido is accomplished in respect of it.'

There are now many reports of children's reactions to the death of a parent. Deutsch (1937) was impressed by the apparent absence in children of overt grief and mourning. Wolfenstein (1966), in a study of 42 children and adolescents who had suffered parent death, stated:

As our observations accumulated we were increasingly struck by the fact that mourning as described by Freud did not occur. Sad feelings were curtailed; there was little weeping. Immersion in the activities of everyday life continued. There was no withdrawal into preoccupation with thoughts of the lost parent.

Gates *et al.* (1965) noted: 'The more adult phenomenon of depression as measured by our criteria does indeed seem minimal in our young children.' Arthur & Kemme (1964) reported that parents were sometimes appalled by their children's lack of concern. Bowlby (1960), on the other hand, contends 'that the responses to be observed in young children on loss of the mother figures differ in no material respect (apart probably from certain consequences) from those observed in adults on loss of a loved object', and 'Like adults, infants and young children who have lost a loved object experience grief and go through periods of mourning' (Bowlby, 1961). Bowlby's remarks are based largely upon his observations of children separated from their mothers in hospital. This is not the same as a child being informed that one of his parents has died.

Three important questions need be asked. (i) To what extent do children comprehend the meaning of death? (ii) If they do comprehend, to what extent can they tolerate the idea of a parent dying? (iii) Are children capable of the painful process of gradual decathexis of libido which characterizes adult grief and mourning?

In the case of a child separated from its mother in hospital the first question is perhaps inappropriate, for, as Robertson (1953) has stated:

To the child of two, with his lack of understanding and complete inability to tolerate frustration, it is really as if his mother had died. He does not know death, but only absence: and if the only person who can satisfy his imperative need is absent, she might as well be dead, so overwhelming is his sense of loss.

In the setting of the bereaved family the child's apparent misconception may lead to considerable confusion and distress. Arthur & Kemme (1964) divided the problem into the concept of the finality of death and that of causality. The problem of finality tended to trouble only those children under age 8. They were convinced that though the parent was dead he was in another place from which he might return. Becker & Margolin (1967), in a study of children under the age of 7, observed: 'Even if told the parent was in heaven the child would say, "What do they do in heaven, what do they wear there, what do they eat?".' The remaining parent was often irritated or upset by the child's suggestion that they might buy or make something for the dead parent and his stubborn unwillingness to accept that the parent would not return. Arthur & Kemme (1964) were struck by the need to blame someone for the death and suggested that this might be explained by Piaget's (1930) observation that the child tends to relate events in the world to his own or other people's wishes.

37

Anthony (1940) devised a series of investigations to demonstrate that the child's concept of death develops as his intellect advances. One involved including the word 'dead' in the vocabulary list of the Revised (1937) Stanford Binet Intelligence Scale. This test was administered to 91 children aged 5 to 13 She observed that as children grow older their definitions of death progress from the very limited meanings such as 'to go to sleep' to those including biological essentials such as 'when you have no pulse and no temperature and can't breathe'. She found that the years 7 to 8 are critical in acquiring a complete comprehension of death. This, according to Piaget (1930, 1932), is when conceptual thinking becomes possible and the child becomes capable of making generalizations. She also found that with maturity and, in a sense, contrary to logic, the child tends to apply the term death specifically to human beings. Thus between 7 and 8 it becomes clearer that death is something which happens to people and is something which could happen to him. She noted that Terman (1916) considered that reference to the human subject, e.g. a chair is 'something you sit on', is a sign of maturity.

It is not easy to differentiate between a child's ability to comprehend death and his ability to tolerate that it has occurred. Bowlby (1961) refers to the defensive process of splitting of the ego. Part of the personality denies that the object is lost, whilst simultaneously another part shares with relatives and friends that it is. Wolfenstein (1966) reported: 'Gradually the fact emerged that overtly or covertly the child was denying the finality of the loss.' She observed that:

All our subjects could state that the parent was in fact dead, and could recall circumstances related to the death such as the funeral. Yet this superficial deference to facts remained isolated from the persistence on another level of expectation of the parent's return.

It would seem that the child desperately clings to the fantasy of the parent still being alive in heaven as an acceptable half-way stage to finally conceding that he is dead in a coffin in the ground.

The third question of whether children are capable of grieving is related to whether they are capable of tolerating the fact that the parent is dead. For even if only part of the personality has denied that the parent is lost forever, the process of detachment of libido from the object in the inner world cannot take place. Deutsch (1937) concluded that such incomplete or unaccomplished mourning in childhood had a disturbing effect upon adult psychic development. Fleming & Altschul (1963) reported the case of a woman of 29 who had lost her parents in middle adolescence, and who had remained fixated at the adolescent level of development until grieving had become possible during analysis. Wolfenstein (1966) suggests that the gradual decathexis of the lost object which protects the mourner from a traumatic release of more unbound libido than he can cope with does not appear to be possible in children and young adolescents. Furman (1964), on the other hand, believes that with assistance even children as young as 4 years old are capable of mourning. He states: 'It is fundamental, however, to make a sharp distinction between a child's not mourning and his incapability of mourning.' His contention is that parents are so disturbed by the pain suffered by the mourning child that they do not permit it to proceed. Hilgard et al. (1960) observed that grief at the death of a parent is recalled only in rare instances when such a death has been experienced prior to the age of nine.

Parents and other adults intuitively feel that children should be spared the facts of parent death. Harrison et al. (1967) showed that adults prefer to distract children from the topic and to deny that the children are upset. They state: 'It should be emphasized, however, that our society has never had much in the way of identifiable guidelines to follow in dealing with children's confrontations with death.' Parents prefer to promote the children's fantasies and delay for a year or more admitting that the parent is buried in the ground. They tend to conceal their own grieving feeling that it would be upsetting to the child. Becker & Margolin (1967) noted that parents admitted that they avoided the topic of the bereavement because they could not bear to face the intensity of their children's feelings. Thus the child's unwillingness to accept the event of death and to grieve over it is reinforced by the protective attitude of adults. Furman (1964) is strongly of the opinion that, though it is an intensely painful process for both child and parent, grieving should be encouraged, though a consistent and unchanging parent substitute should be available.

The evidence of Deutsch (1937) and Fleming & Altschul (1963) noted above would suggest that because of the restriction of the mourning process in children there might be a greater tendency to psychiatric illness in adults who have suffered early parent death. Bowlby (1961) states: 'As in the case, say, of rheumatic fever, scar tissue is all too often formed which in later life leads to more or less severe dysfunction.' Brown (1961) expresses a similar view: 'It may well be that this type of trauma is likely to produce a nucleus of depressive affect which can be re-stimulated by subsequent rejections in much later life.' A large number of studies have compared the incidence of early parent death in psychiatric patients and in the general population. The findings of such studies are conflicting. Brown (1961) demonstrated a high incidence of early parent death in depressed patients. Munro (1966) did not. Using the MMPI, Archibald *et al.* (1962) and Gregory (1966) failed to show a predominance of depressive symptomatology in patients who had suffered early parent death.

Parent death and the oedipal conflict

During oedipal development the child competes with the parent of his own sex for the affection of the other parent. When the parent of the same sex dies he has what he has always longed for, the parent of the opposite sex to himself. He cannot enjoy this victory for, as Fenichel (1931) has pointed out, he is overcome by the guilt engendered by the fantasy fulfilment of his murderous wishes towards this parent. Arthur & Kemme (1964) observed such guilt reactions in the majority of 49 children who suffered the death of the same-sexed parent. In 13 the behaviour was 'either directly or symbolically self-punitive or provoked and invited punishment from others'. Fast & Cain (1963) observed in sons who lost their fathers 'intense attempts to avoid positive feelings for the mothers and fervent feelings of loyalty to the dead father'. One boy had idyllic daydreams about his mother combined with fears of castration as a retribution from his father. Intense jealousy may arise if the remaining parent seeks a replacement by forming new sexual relationships outside the family. Wolfenstein (1966) has proposed that the child may interpret the parent's grief as rejection of his incestuous strivings and experience anew his inability to compete with the dead parent. A boy reported by Meiss (1952) suffered from insomnia, for he believed that each night his mother met his dead father in 'Cockadoodle Land'. He also had anxieties that she might die and reunite with his father forever in death.

Death of a parent of the opposite sex represents the removal of the most coveted object. Even though the parent is dead the child is reluctant to relinquish his libidinal attachment. He may transform this defeat into a victory and, by establishing an intensified fantasy relationship, proclaim that the parent is now exclusively his forever (Fenichel, 1931).

Idealization of the dead parent of the opposite sex was observed by Arthur & Kemme
(1964) in 15 of 34 children who suffered such
loss. It was particularly marked in girls, who
strongly resented attempts to intrude upon or
devalue the fantasy relationship with their
fathers. All negative feelings towards the
dead parent are denied and tend to be pro-
jected upon the remaining parent, who is seen
as bad and responsible for the parent's
death. Jacobson (1965) has compared the
striving to recover the parent with the small
girl's longing to recover her lost penis, and
considers this may account for the guilt
which is sometimes present. Suicide may be
contemplated or attempted as a reunion in
death with the parent. An unwillingness to
abandon the fantasy relationship results in an
inability to enter into satisfactory heterosexual
relationships in the real world. There is a
tendency to form libidinized attachments to
substitute figures but, as in the case reported
by Neubauer (1960) who transferred the
idealization to her stepfather, such relationships are not subjected to reality testing.

Successful resolution of the oedipal situation is impaired by the subsequent relationship which develops between the child and the
remaining parent. 'When bereaved of the
adult who offered important emotional satisfactions both parent and child are frequently
tempted to turn to one another for substitute
gratification' (Fast & Cain, 1963). Wolfenstein (1966) noted that in many instances the
widowed parent arranged for the child to
share the same bedroom or even the same
bed and numerous unconvincing rationaliza-
tions were offered for this. The effects of this
differ according to the sex of the parent lost.
When the parent of the opposite sex dies a
strong homosexual bond may form between
the child and the remaining parent. This may
be due to the guilt engendered by persistent
longing for the dead parent or as Neubauer

(1960) has suggested, an inhibition of the normal oedipal hostility towards the same-sexed parent due to the dependence of the child upon the only available love object. In a sense the child has accepted the remaining parent as a substitute for the one that is lost. This process is facilitated by the fact that this parent may in reality need to assume some of the roles of the lost parent.

When the parent of the same sex dies there is a tendency for the remaining parent to seduce the child. Though this may be interpreted as a simple transference of libido from spouse to child, it may be that the parent of the same sex when alive, not only inhibits the child's oedipal longings but also the seductive impulses of the opposite sexed parent. Attempts to ward off the now unrestrained incestuous feelings may result in the parent's loathing the child and favouring a sibling of the opposite sex as a form of expiation. Hilgard *et al.* (1960), in a study of adults who had suffered the death of a father in childhood, observed that

several men felt as though their mother had placed them in the position of substitute husbands, and in our review of the material it seems to us that this had frequently been the case whether the son verbalized it or not.

Prugh & Harlow (1962) described a mother whose son so resembled his dead father that she could relate to him only through her identification of him with her husband. As her own father died when she was a child, her denial of her husband's death was also a denial of her father's death.

Freud (1905) proposed that the seduction of a son by his mother was one cause of homosexuality. He, like Ferenczi (1914), was of the opinion that the competitive relationship with the father had the effect of deflecting libido from his own sex. O'Connor (1964) observed that 24 per cent of 50 male homosexuals compared with 2 per cent of 50 neurotics reported their fathers to be away from home for a long period during childhood or adolescence and 62 per cent compared with 8 per cent of neurotics were more attached to their mothers than to their fathers. Kaye *et al.* (1967), in a study of 24 female homosexual patients and 24 controls, concluded that the fathers of the homosexuals tended to be possessive and close-binding. Thus the absence of the same-sexed parent coupled by an intensified relationship with the opposite sexed parent may create guilt about all heterosexual desires.

Meiss (1952) emphasizes the need for objects of both sexes when the integrative tasks of the oedipal period are at their height. Neubauer (1960) considers the timing of the parent death to be important. From a survey of 10 reported cases he concluded that the death of the parent fixates the oedipal rivalry and prevents successful resolution of the conflict.

Parent death and the problems of identification

Lynn (1962) is careful to distinguish between sex-role identification and parental identification. The former refers to the internalisation of the role considered appropriate to a given sex and to the unconcsious reactions characteristic of that role. The latter refers to the internalization of personality characteristics of one's own parent and to unconscious reactions similar to that parent. It is possible to identify with a parent of either sex and even if one identifies with a parent of the same sex that parent's sexual identity may be poor or even reversed.

Recent research on hermaphroditism has clearly demonstrated that sex-role identification can be contrary to both chromosomal sex and gonadal sex. Brown & Lynn (1966) point out that 'Individuals of comparable anatomical and physiological deviation in

44

composition have been reared successfully as either boys or girls.' Brown (1958) believes that sex-role differentiation is a gradual process beginning some time after the first year and becoming complete and irreversible around the fifth year. He likens it to imprinting in lower animals. The absence of the appropriate sexed parent during this critical period may impair such 'gender imprinting'.

Brown & Lynn (1966) further differentiate between sex-role identification, sex-role preference and sex-role adoption. A person may identify with one sex but prefer to be the other or adopt the behaviour of the other. Parsons & Bales (1955) consider the family of orientation as split vertically by sex and horizontally by generation. The child perceives himself as belonging to one sexual and one generational category and learns the behaviour appropriate to this category. Such learning depends to a large extent upon the process of identification with parents. Lynn (1961) has pointed out that children of both sexes identify initially with the mother but that boys must eventually shift their identification to the father. For this reason boys experience greater difficulty in establishing a correct sexual identity and are more vulnerable to disturbances in family organization. The studies of Bach (1946), Sears (1951) and Stolz (1954) of children whose fathers were absent through World War II showed that, compared with children brought up in intact households, the boys were more effeminate and less aggressive and resembled more closely the girls both in behaviour and fantasy. Lynn & Sawrey (1959), in a study of Norwegian children whose fathers were away at sea for long periods, showed the boys to make stronger strivings for father identification and react to their insecure masculine identification with compensatory masculinity.

The normal process of acquiring satisfactory sexual identity may be impaired by

45

parent death. This is due both to the absence of the parent as a model and to the emotional responses consequent upon the parent's death. Identification with the lost object is a feature of adult grief but in children it is commoner and usually takes a more dramatic form, as shown by Shambaugh (1961), Barnes (1964), Gauthier (1965) and Laufer (1966). Identification occurs irrespective of the sex of the parent lost. Such a reaction is probably an attempt to deny the loss. It is as though the child is saying: 'My father is alive because I am he.' Eisendorfer (1943) believes that identification with the lost parent is an important condition for being loved by the surviving parent. The intensity of the relationship with the remaining parent may in part be due to such identification.

Arthur & Kemme (1964) have pointed out that when the parent of the same sex has died there appears to be conflict over identification partly due to fears of vulnerability of members of the same sex and partly due to guilt over incestuous impulses. Boys tend to be effeminate and girls to be 'tom boys'.

The effect of parent death on familial equilibrium

For most young animals the period of immaturity is relatively short. They grow up quickly, for in the wild there are many dangers and food is scarce. Family organization is simple and is usually restricted to the mother and the siblings. However, Harlow (1961) has shown that, in monkeys, replacement of the mother with a cloth surrogate results in failure to show normal sexual behaviour. The human infant is born into the relatively complex family of orientation. The family members constitute the household; they live together in a house which they regard as home. Usually they are surrounded by neighbours, in a neighbourhood, which is part of their home town. The family unit is maintained in a state of equilibrium by conventions, taboos and inhibitions. The older members, being wiser and experienced, are respected and obeyed. They provide security, set examples, hold power, punish and reward. The father represents male sexuality and is the main source of income, social status, authority and discipline. The mother represents female sexuality and is the main source of tenderness and affection. It is accepted that overt sexual behaviour occurs only between father and mother, though sexual relationships exist between all family members. The functions of the family (Parsons & Bales, 1955) are (i) the socialization of the child, so that he can become a member of the society into which he has been born and (ii) the stabilization of the adult personality. As Cumming (1961) has expressed it: 'The family of orientation must, like other socializing institutions, be resigned to expelling its members when their socialization reaches an adequate level.' The younger members come to acquire independent identities, argue with and defy their parents until they escape into familiar limbo. This breaking free inevitably involves detachment of libido and in this sense is analogous to mourning, though, as Wolfenstein (1966) has pointed out, when the adolescent's withdrawl becomes too difficult, he can temporarily return to his parents.

It might be suspected that following death of a parent breaking away from the family of orientation may be more difficult and may be imperfectly accomplished. Archibald et al. (1962) gained the impression that men who had lost mothers expressed unusual dependency and hostility in their marital relationships. Barry et al. (1965) observed that dependency was a prominent characteristic of 13 of 15 subjects whose mothers had died between the age of 3 months and 4 years, but of only four of 15 subjects whose mothers had

47

died between the ages of 11 and 17 years. The early bereaved group 'typically showed a wistful, insistent clinging to the doctors, nurses or other key figures for support and affection'. This effect is due in part to the attitude of the remaining parent. Hilgard *et al.* (1960) noted that:

In one form of social pathology, the surviving parent becomes so emotionally dependent upon the children that the child finds it difficult to make a normal separation from the parent when he himself becomes an adult.

Burton & Whiting (1961), reviewing studies of Norwegian sailors' families, where the father was often absent for two or more years, found that the mothers were over-protective and the boys tended to be infantile and dependent.

An older sibling may either assume or be seen to assume the role of the dead parent. Rosenbaum (1963), citing the examples of a boy cared for by an older brother, and a girl cared for by an older sister, showed that in the absence of a controlling parent sibling rivalry may be intense. He pointed out that:

The adult, having gone through the biological experience of motherhood, possesses the instincts and behavioural capacity for mothering that must, to some degree at least, temper the hostile and aggressive impulses towards the helpless child, wanted or unwanted. But in an older sibling, regardless of how normal he may be, the ambivalent feelings towards the younger sibling were intense with the most destructive fantasies and impulses human beings possess.

Ekstein, in the discussion of the same paper, described the savage assaults of an aunt upon a girl whose father had deserted and whose mother was chronically hospitalized. It was considered that this hostility was displaced hatred of her sister whom she had tried to mother for many years. When libidinal displacement on to an older sibling occurs, a damaging incestuous relationship may result

48

and intense jealousy may emerge at the loved sibling's marriage.

The introduction of a step-parent creates problems for the children and the remaining parent. These have been described by Fast & Cain (1966). The remaining parent may be unwilling to withdraw libido from the dead spouse. The children too may maintain a relationship with the idealized natural parent. The parent may be reluctant to permit and the children to accept discipline or punishment from the step-parent. Failure to establish a true generational barrier and incest taboo facilitates the development of sexual relationships between step-parent and children, generates anxieties about such relationships in the parent and leads to competition between the parent and children of the same sex for the step-parent. Conversely, as the step-parent is less threatening than the natural parent oedipal relationships between the remaining parent and children of the opposite sex arouse less guilt and are strengthened by unfavourable comparisons with the dead parent. For the same reason identification with the step-parent may not be possible.

Conclusions

In the studies reviewed there has been a gradual transition from the consideration of parent death as a separation of the child from a loved object to the consideration of it as a disorganization of the relationships within the family unit. The various disturbances of the familial equilibrium have been observed to depend upon (i) the special relationship which existed between the lost parent and the child, (ii) the relationships which existed between the parent and the other family members, (iii) the controlling influence the parent exerted upon other relationships within the family, (iv) the influence other family members exerted upon the relationship which existed between the child and the lost parent and (v) the influence the child exerted upon relationships which existed between the lost parent and the other family members.

The primary disturbance remains that of the relationship which existed between the parent and the child, whatever the sex of the child and whatever the sex of the parent lost. The relationship with each parent in the real world is reflected by the libidinal attachment to the internalized parental object. As Sandler & Joffe (1965) have emphasized, this attachment is a source of well-being to the child and will not be readily relinquished even though the relationship to the parent in the real world has ceased to exist. This discrepancy between outer and inner reality may be perpetuated over a number of years.

Whether satisfactory decathexis of the loved object takes place is conditional upon (i) the preparedness of the child, his level of maturity and ego development, (ii) the attitude of the remaining parent or other adults, their ability to comprehend their irrational anxieties and hostilities and their tolerance of such emotions in the child, (iii) the denial mechanisms of the child and the protection devices of the remaining parent, (iv) the oedipal significance of the lost parent for the child and the effect of this on his relationship with the remaining parent, and (v) the availability and consistency of a replacement parent figure.

REFERENCES

ANDRY, R. (1955). A comparative psychological study of parent-child relationships as associated with delinquency. (Unpublished thesis, University of London.)

ANTHONY, S. (1940). *The Child's Discovery of Death*. London: Kegan Paul, Trench Trubner.

ARCHIBALD, H. *et al.* (1962). Bereavement in childhood and adult psychiatric disturbance. *Psychosom. Med.* **24**, 343–351.

ARTHUR, B. & KEMME, M. (1964). Bereavement in childhood. *J. child Psychol. Psychiat.* **5**, 37–49.

BACH, G. (1946). Father-fantasies and father-typing in father-separated children. *Child Dev.* **17**, 63–80.

BARNES, M. (1964). Reactions to the death of a mother. *Psychoanal. Study Child* **19**, 334–357.

BARRY, H. Jr., BARRY, H. III & LINDEMANN, E. (1965). Dependency in adult patients following early maternal bereavement. *J. nerv. ment. Dis.* **140**, 196–206.

BECKER, D. & MARGOLIN, F. (1967). How surviving parents handled their young children's adaptation to the crisis of loss. *Am. J. Orthopsychiat.* **37**, 753–757.

BOWLBY, J. (1946). *Forty-Four Juvenile Thieves, their Character and Home Life.* London: Baillière, Tindall & Cox.

BOWLBY, J. (1951). *Maternal Care and Mental Health.* Geneva: W.H.O.

BOWLBY, J. (1960). Grief and mourning in infancy and early childhood. *Psychoanal. Study Child* **15**, 9–52.

BOWLBY, J. (1961). Childhood mourning and its implications for psychiatry. *Am. J. Psychiat.* **118**, 481–498.

BOWLBY, J., AINSWORTH, M., BOSTON, M. & ROSENBLUTH, D. (1956). The effects of mother–child separation: a follow-up study. *Br. J. med. Psychol.* **29**, 211–244.

BROWN, D. (1958). Sex-role developement in a changing culture. *Psychol. Bull.* **54**, 232–242.

BROWN, D. & LYNN, D. (1966). Human sexual development: an outline of components and concepts. *J. Marriage Family* **28**, 155–162.

BROWN, F. (1961). Depression and childhood bereavement. *J. ment. Sci.* **107**, 754–777.

BROWN, F. & EPPS, P. (1966). Childhood bereavement and subsequent crime. *Br. J. Psychiat.* **112**, 1043–1048.

BURLINGHAM, D. & FREUD, A. (1944). *Infants Without Families.* London: Allen & Unwin.

BURTON, R. & WHITING, J. (1961). The absent father and cross-sex identity. *Merrill–Palmer Q. Behav. Dev.* **7**, 85–95.

CUMMING, J. (1961). The family and mental disorders: an incomplete essay. In *Causes of Mental Disorders: A Review of Epidemiological Knowledge, 1959.* Millbank Memorial Fund.

DEUTSCH, H. (1937). Absence of grief. *Psychoanal. Q.* **6**, 12–22.

EISENDORFER, A. (1943). The clinical significance of the single parent relationship in women. *Psychoanal. Q.* **12**, 223–239.

ENGEL, G. (1961). Is grief a disease? *Psychosom. Med.* **23**, 18–22.

FAST, I. & CAIN, A. (1963). Disturbances in parent–child relationships following bereavement. (Paper read to American Psychological Association.)

FAST, I. & CAIN, A. (1966). The step-parent role: potential for disturbances in family functioning. *Am. J. Orthopsychiat.* **36**, 485–491.

FENICHEL, O. (1931). Specific forms of the oedipus complex. In H. Fenichel & D. Rapaport (eds.), *The Collected Papers of Otto Fenichel*, vol. 1. New York: Norton, 1953.

FERENCZI, S. (1914). The nosology of male homosexuality (homoerotism). In *Sex in Psychoanalysis.* New York: Basic Books, 1950.

FLEMING, J. & ALTSCHUL, S. (1963). Activation of mourning and growth by psychoanalysis. *Int. J. Psycho-Anal.* **44**, 419–431.

FREUD, A. (1960). Discussion of Dr John Bowlby's paper. *Psychoanal. Study Child* **15**, 53–62.

FREUD, S. (1905). Three essays on the theory of sexuality. *Standard Edition*, vol. 7, pp. 123–245. London: Hogarth Press, 1953.

FREUD, S. (1917). Mourning and melancholia. *Standard Edition*, vol. 14, pp. 237–260. London: Hogarth Press, 1957.

FURMAN, R. (1964). Death and the young child. *Psychoanal. Study Child* **19**, 321–333.

GATES, P., ROFF, C. & STIVER, I. (1965). Studies of the significance of death of a parent for young children: a preliminary report. (Paper read to 42nd Annual Meeting of the American Orthopsychiatric Association.)

GAUTHIER, Y. (1965). The mourning reaction of a ten-and-a-half-year-old boy. *Psychoanal. Study Child* **20**, 481–494.

GLUECK, S. & GLUECK, E. (1950). *Unravelling*

Juvenile Delinquency. Harvard University Press.

GOLDFARB, W. (1943*a*). Effects of early institutional care on adolescent personality. *J. exp. Educ.* **12**, 106–129.

GOLDFARB, W. (1943*b*). The effects of early institutional care on adolescent personality. *Child Dev.* **14**, 213–223.

GOLDFARB, W. (1944). Effects of early institutional care on adolescent personality: Rorschach data. *Am. J. Orthopsychiat.* **14**, 441–447.

GOLDFARB, W. (1947). Variations in adolescent adjustment in institutionally reared children. *Am. J. Orthopsychiat.* **17**, 449–457.

GREGORY, I. (1966). Retrospective data concerning childhood loss of a parent. *Archs gen. Psychiat.* **15**, 362–367.

HARLOW, H. (1961). *Mother–Infant Interactions of Monkeys*. London: Tavistock Study Group on Mother–Infant Interaction.

HARRISON, S., DAVENPORT, C. & MCDERMOTT, J. (1967). Children's reactions to bereavement. *Archs gen. Psychiat.* **17**, 593–597.

HILGARD, J., NEWMAN, M. & FISK, F. (1960). Strength of adult ego following childhood bereavement. *Am. J. Orthopsychiat.* **30**, 788–798.

HOWELLS, J. (1959). Children in hospital. *Br. med. J.* **1**, 1119.

JACOBSON, E. (1965). The return of the lost parent. In M. Schur (ed.), *Drives, Affects, Behavior*, vol. 2, pp. 193–211. New York: International Universities Press.

KAYE, H. *et al.* (1967). Homosexuality in women. *Archs gen. Psychiat.* **17**, 626–634.

LAUFER, M. (1966). Object loss and mourning during adolescence. *Psychoanal. Study Child* **21**, 269–293.

LEVY, D. (1937). Primary affect hunger. *Am. J. Psychiat.* **94**, 643–652.

LEWIS, H. (1954). *Deprived Children (The Mersham Experiment): a Social and Clinical Study*. London: Oxford University Press.

LINDEMANN, E. (1944). Symptomatology and management of acute grief. *Am. J. Psychiat.* **101**, 141–148.

LYNN, D. (1961). Sex differences in identification development. *Sociometry* **24**, 372–383.

LYNN, D. (1962). Sex-role and parental identification. *Child Dev.* **33**, 555–564.

LYNN, D. & SAWREY, W. (1959). The effects of father-absence on Norwegian boys and girls. *J. abnorm. soc. Psychol.* **59**, 258–262.

MAHLER, M. (1961). On sadness and grief in infancy and childhood. *Psychoanal. Study Child* **16**, 332–351.

MEISS, M. (1952). The oedipal problem of a fatherless child. *Psychoanal. Study Child* **7**, 216–229.

MUNRO, A. (1965). Childhood parent-loss in a psychiatrically normal population. *Br. J. prev. soc. Med.* **19**, 69–79.

MUNRO, A. (1966). Parental deprivation in depressive patients. *Br. J. Psychiat.* **112**, 443–457.

NEUBAUER, P. (1960). The one-parent child and his oedipal development. *Psychoanal. Study Child* **15**, 286–309.

O'CONNOR, P. (1964). Aetiological factors in homosexuality as seen in Royal Air Force psychiatric practice. *Br. J. Psychiat.* **110**, 381–391.

PARSONS, T. & BALES, R. (1955). *Family Socialization and Interaction Process.* Glencoe, Ill.: Free Press.

PIAGET, J. (1930). *The Child's Conception of Physical Causality.* New York: Harcourt, Brace.

PIAGET, J. (1932). *The Language and Thought of the Child.* New York: Harcourt, Brace.

PRUGH, D. & HARLOW, R. (1962). 'Masked deprivation' in infants and young children. In *Deprivation of Maternal Care: a Reassessment of its Effects.* (Public Health Papers, 14.) Geneva: W.H.O.

ROBERTSON, J. (1953). Some responses of young children to the loss of maternal care. *Nursing Times* **49**, 382–386.

ROSENBAUM, M. (1963). Psychological effects on the child raised by an older sibling. *Am. J. Orthopsychiat.* **33**, 515–520.

SANDLER, J. & JOFFE, W (1965). Notes on childhood depression. *Int. J. Psycho-Anal.* **46**, 88–96.

SEARS, P. (1951). Doll play aggression in normal young children: influence of sex, age, sibling status, father absence. *Psychol. Monogr.* **65**, no. 6. (Whole no. 323.)

SHAMBAUGH, B. (1961). A study of loss reactions in a seven-year-old. *Psychoanal. Study Child* **16**, 510–522.

SPITZ, R. A. (1945). Hospitalism. *Psychoanal. Study Child* 1, 53–74.

SPITZ, R. A. (1946). Hospitalism: a follow-up report. *Psychoanal. Study Child* 2, 113–117.

SPITZ, R. A. (1949). The role of ecological factors in emotional developments in infancy. *Child Dev.* 20, 145–155.

STOLZ, L. (1954). *Father Relation of Warborn Children*. Palo Alto: Stanford University Press.

SUTHERLAND, E. (1934). *Principles of Criminology*, rev. ed. Philadelphia.

TERMAN, L. (1916). *The Measurement of Intelligence*. Boston: Houghton Mifflin.

WOLFENSTEIN, M. (1966). How is mourning possible? *Psychoanal. Study Child* 21, 93–123.

WOOTON, B. (1962). A social scientist's approach to maternal deprivation. In *Deprivation of Maternal Care: a Reassessment of its Effects*. (Public Health Papers, 14.) Geneva: W.H.O.

WRETMARK, G. (1959). A study of grief reactions. *Acta psychiat. scand.* 34, Suppl. 292–299.

Early Parent Death and Mental Illness

By JOHN BIRTCHNELL

Environmentalists have long attempted to demonstrate relationships between various deficiencies in upbringing and adult mental illness. Early parent death is one of the most obvious and one of the most easily measured of such deficiencies, and many investigators have been tempted to the deceptively simple task of comparing the incidence of early parent death in patients and the general population. That there is so little agreement in the findings of the now considerable number of studies is a reflection of the methodological pitfalls which exist.

As Dennehy (1966) has rightly pointed out, "the problem of control groups is crucial", and it is in this area that so many of the methodological difficulties have arisen.

In the present investigation a control group has been obtained from the local population by the method of postal questionnaires. Such a control group has the advantages of being unselected, inasmuch as the subjects were not seeking medical attention, though inevitably some were receiving it, and of representing closely the psychiatric patient group. It has been possible to estimate the incidence of early parent death in the patient and the control group in respect of the following factors:

(*i*) the sex of the parent lost,

(*ii*) the sex of the bereaved,

(*iii*) the year of loss,

(*iv*) the current age of the bereaved,

(*v*) the age of the parent at the birth of the bereaved.

METHOD

(i) *Psychiatric Patient Group*

The psychiatric patients comprise 100 consecutive admissions to the Crichton Royal Hospital, Dumfries, for the years 1959, 1960, 1961, 1962 and 1963, providing a case had not been included in a group for a previous year. The sample included only those normally resident in the hospital catchment area— Dumfriesshire, Kirkcudbrightshire and Wigtownshire—and those aged between 20 and 59. Both amenity and non-amenity patients were included, there being 90 amenity patients.

All genuine psychiatric patients were included; the diagnostic breakdown is given in Table I. The sample included both first admissions and readmissions.

Of the 500 cases, information was lacking on 150. A short letter and simple questionnaire was sent to these patients, followed by a reminder letter to those who had not replied. The remaining patients were visited by their mental welfare officers. Finally there remained 4 patients with information lacking for both parents and 14 patients with information lacking for father only. Thus complete information was available for 482 patients (96 per cent). In all calculations the cases with missing information have been excluded.

TABLE I
Diagnostic Breakdown of the Psychiatric Patient Group

Diagnosis	Men	Women	Total
Depression (all types)	77	182	259
Schizophrenia	32	33	65
Alcoholism	57	11	68
Psychopathy or Behaviour Disorder ..	32	12	44
Neurosis (excluding depression) ..	8	11	19
Mania or Hypomania	6	8	14
Others	20	11	31
Total	232	268	500

57

(ii) *Dumfriesshire Control Group*

The Royal College of General Practitioners supplied the name of a local doctor who kept an age/sex register. The practice was in the small town of Langholm, Dumfriesshire (population 2,360) and included a number of surrounding villages. It was considered to represent the hospital catchment area as a whole. From the age/sex register, a group of 500 individuals, matched for age and sex with the patient group were selected. A brief explanatory letter with a questionnaire was sent, together with a stamped addressed envelope for reply to the G.P. Two reminder letters were sent after one week and a fortnight. Replies were carefully written and the final response was 476 (95 per cent.). In a small proportion of cases the date of birth stated by the patient was different from that recorded by the G.P. The age and sex distribution of the patient and the control group is given in Table II.

(iii) *Social Class*

The patient and control group have not been matched for social class. As the Crichton Royal Hospital provides adequate amenity accommodation, and as there is no private psychiatric practice in the hospital catchment area, Social Class I and II patients are well represented. In parent death studies matching for social class is particularly difficult, as it is the social class of the parents which must be matched for and for various reasons the social class of the patients cannot be accepted as a reflection of that of the parents.

(iv) *Presentation of Results*

Parent death, in all cases, refers to the natural parent and not to a step-parent or person who has come to be looked upon as a parent. A statement stressing this was made in the questionnaires. Where two parents have died during the period of childhood, the earliest death has been counted and used in the calculations but a note has been made of the second death in a separate column. This is because, as it is the stress of bereavement which is being considered, it is preferable to measure the number of individuals who have suffered parent death rather than the number of parents who have died. For this reason, when two parents have died in the same year ·5 is counted under both father deaths and mother deaths.

When illegitimacy is recorded this is listed separately. On the questionnaires the statement "if you have never known your father/mother write

Table II

Age and Sex Distribution of the Patient and the Control Group. The Distribution of the Control Group is that of Those Who Returned Completed Questionnaires. The Three Cases Age 60 to 64 have been Excluded from All Calculations. For Comparison, the Distribution of the Patient Group is that of Cases for Which Information about Both Parents is Known

Age in 1963	Patients			Controls		
	Men	Women	Total	Men	Women	Total
20–24	19	24	43	17	24	41
25–29	21	16	37	21	17	38
30–34	25	22	47	27	23	50
35–39	32	42	74	31	41	72
40–44	36	35	71	39	39	78
45–49	22	41	63	21	39	60
50–54	33	34	67	29	26	55
55–59	35	45	80	33	46	79
60–64	0	0	0	2	1	3
Total	223	259	482	220	256	476

'never known' in the answer column", was included. No one wrote "never known" for mothers, and all cases answering "never known" for fathers have been included as illegitimate, though perhaps some of these were in fact early desertions. It is suspected that in some studies the rather high incidence of very early father deaths is due to the inclusion of masked illegitimates. A child with unmarried parents living together has not been considered as illegitimate.

There are two ways of expressing the incidence. It may be expressed as a percentage of the total known cases or as a percentage of the number of cases remaining capable of losing the particular parent, i.e. with the parent still alive. In the second method all cases whose parents were known to have died before the age-span considered are subtracted from the denominator. The first method has been adopted throughout, and in calculations the larger denominator has been used.

RESULTS

The Relationship Between Early Parent Death and Age

Table III provides a comparison, for patients and controls, of the incidence of early parent death in those aged 20 to 39 and 40 to 59. It will be seen that in the control group the incidence of early parent death is significantly higher in those aged over 40 ($p < \cdot 01$). In the patient group, though there is a similar difference it is not a significant one.

This less definite relationship with age would appear to be due to the fact that the incidence of early parent death in the patients under age 40 ($25 \cdot 3$ per cent.) is significantly higher than that in the controls under age 40 ($16 \cdot 9$ per cent.). The incidences in patients and controls over age 40 ($32 \cdot 2$ per cent. and $29 \cdot 8$ per cent. respectively) correspond more closely.

Consideration of Age at Loss, Sex of Parent Lost and Sex of Bereaved

Tables IV and V show the incidence of parent death by five-year age-spans for patients and controls. When the complete period from age 0 to 19 is considered, it will be seen that the incidence of parent death in the two groups, $29 \cdot 9$ per cent. for the patients and $24 \cdot 3$ per cent. for the controls, is similar. Mother deaths

TABLE III

The Incidence of Parent Death Occurring Before Age 20 in Relation to the Sex of the Parent Lost for Subjects Younger and Older than Age 40 in 1963

Age in 1963	Patients						Controls					
	Father		Mother		Either		Father		Mother		Either	
	Deaths	Total known	Deaths	Total known	Deaths	Total known	Deaths	Total known	Deaths	Total known	Deaths	Total known
20–39 ..	30 (14·9%)	201	22 (10·6%)	207	52 (25·5%)	204*	19 (9·5%)	201	15 (7·5%)	201	34 (16·9%)	201
40–49 ..	57·5 (20·5%)	281	34·5 (11·9%)	289	92 (32·4%)	285*	45·5 (16·7%)	272	35·5 (13·1%)	272	81 (29·8%)	272
Total ..	87·5 (18·1%)	482	56·5 (11·4%)	496	144 (29·4%)	489*	64·5 (13·6%)	473	50·5 (10·7%)	473	115 (24·3%)	473

Death of either parent age 0 to 19, patients: controls (20 to 39) $\chi^2 = 4·451$, d.f. $= 1$, p $< ·05$
Death of either parent age 0 to 19, patients: controls (40 to 59) $\chi^2 = 0·407$, d.f. $= 1$, N.S.
Death of either parent age 0 to 19, 20 to 39: 40 to 59 (controls) $\chi^2 = 10·394$, d.f. $= 1$, p $< ·01$
Death of either parent age 0 to 19, 20 to 39: 40 to 59 (patients) $\chi^2 = 2·639$, d.f. $= 1$, N.S.

* As the denominator for father deaths is included in that for mother deaths, the denominator for death of either parent is obtained by adding half the difference between the two parent denominators to that for father deaths. This in effect is the mean of the two parent denominators.

61

in particular are almost the same. When the period from age 0 to 9 is considered, a more marked and now significant difference between patients and controls becomes apparent— 17·7 per cent. against 11·3 per cent. This difference is most marked for father deaths, which considered alone are significant at the ·05 level. Loss by daughters is greater than loss by sons, and daughter losses considered separately are significant at the ·02 level. The age period when the difference between patients and controls is most striking is that from age 0 to 4. During this period 9·8 per cent. of patients and 4·7 per cent. of controls suffered parent death. Father deaths and mother deaths considered separately are both significant at the ·05 level. Again loss by daughters is greater and is significant at the ·02 level.

Consideration of Age of the Parent at Birth of the Subject

Those born to elderly parents are more likely to suffer early parent death than those born to young parents. It is important therefore to ascertain whether the differences between patients and controls in respect of early parent death can be attributed to differences in the parental age at birth. Table VI shows the mean ages at birth for parents who died before the subject was 20. The differences are small and not significant.

Diagnosis

As approximately half the patient group are depressives, the numbers included in other diagnostic groups are small. Thus consideration of the relationship between early parent death and diagnosis is limited. It has been shown that the diagnostic distribution of the 85 patients who suffered parent death before age 10 did not differ significantly from the expected.

DISCUSSION

A serious defect of a number of studies is the failure to consider the incidence of early parent death in adequate detail. This is particularly so in respect of the year of loss. High incidences

Table IV

The Incidence of Parent Death by Five-Year Age-Spans up to Age 20 and Illegitimacy for the Dumfriesshire Control Sample, Considering Separately the Sex of the Bereaved and the Sex of the Parent Lost. The Percentages are the Percentages of Known Cases

Age at death of parent	Father		Mother		Either parent	Second death		Illegitimate plus mother death
	Daughters	Sons	Daughters	Sons		Father	Mother	
0–4	7.5 (3.0%)	3 (1.4%)	6.5 (2.6%)	5 (2.3%)	22 (4.7%)	0	2	1
5–9	7 (2.8%)	10 (4.6%)	7 (2.8%)	7 (3.2%)	31 (6.6%)	0	2	2
10–14	11 (4.3%)	6 (2.7%)	8 (3.1%)	7 (3.2%)	32 (6.8%)	1	2	1
15–19	9 (3.5%)	11 (5.0%)	6 (2.4%)	4 (1.8%)	30 (6.3%)	5	1	0
Total early parent death	34.5 (13.6%)	30 (13.7%)	27.5 (10.8%)	23 (10.5%)	115 (24.3%)	6	7	4
Illegitimates mother alive	15 (5.9%)	11 (5.0%)	—	—	26			
Not known	12 (4.5%)	12 (5.2%)	12 (4.5%)	12 (5.2%)	24 (4.8%)			
Group Total	266	231	266	231	497			

TABLE V

The Incidence of Parent Death by Five-Year Age-Spans up to Age 20 and Illegitimacy for the Crichton Royal Patients, Considering Separately the Sex of the Bereaved and the Sex of the Parent Lost. The Percentages are the Percentages of Known Cases

Age at death of parent	Father		Mother		Either parent	Second death		Illegitimate plus mother death
	Daughters	Sons	Daughters	Sons		Father	Mother	
0–4	15.5 (6.0%)	6.5 (2.9%)	14.5 (5.5%)	10.5 (4.6%)	47 (9.8%)	1	5	3
5–9	11.5 (4.4%)	12 (5.4%)	7.5 (2.8%)	7 (3.0%)	38 (7.9%)	1	1	1
10–14	7 (2.7%)	11 (4.9%)	9 (3.4%)	1 (0.4%)	28 (5.8%)	4	3	0
15–19	13 (5.0%)	11 (4.9%)	4 (1.5%)	3 (1.3%)	31 (6.4%)	3	3	0
Total early parent death	47 (18.0%)	40.5 (18.0%)	35 (13.1%)	21.5 (9.3%)	144 (29.9%)	9	12	4
Illegitimates mother alive	19 (7.3%)	18 (8.0%)	—	—	37			
Not known	9 (3.4%)	9 (3.9%)	2 (0.7%)	2 (0.9%)	18			
Group Total	268	232	268	232	500			

Chi Square comparison with control figures (Table IV)

Father deaths	Age 0 to 4	$x^2 = 3.896$	d.f. = 1	p < .05	Age 0 to 9	$x^2 = 4.291$	d.f. = 1	p < .05
Mother deaths	Age 0 to 4	$x^2 = 4.547$	d.f. = 1	p < .05	Age 0 to 9	$x^2 = 2.561$	d.f. = 1	N.S.
Death of either parent	Age 0 to 4	$x^2 = 8.780$	d.f. = 1	p < .01	Age 0 to 9	$x^2 = 7.324$	d.f. = 1	p < .01
Son losses	Age 0 to 4	$x^2 = 2.866$	d.f. = 1	N.S.	Age 0 to 9	$x^2 = 1.573$	d.f. = 1	N.S.
Daughter losses	Age 0 to 4	$x^2 = 5.517$	d.f. = 1	p < .02	Age 0 to 9	$x^2 = 5.551$	d.f. = 1	p < .02

during early years can be cancelled out by lower incidences during later years, so that the total incidences prior to a certain age may be similar for patients and controls.

In the present study, death of a parent during the period from birth to age 20 was shown not to be excessive in the patient group. Consideration of the period prior to age 10 revealed significant differences between patients and controls, suggesting that death of a parent during this period is an aetiological factor. The differences between patients and controls were even more striking during the period prior to age 5. A number of investigators (Pitts *et al.*, 1965; Brill and Liston, 1966; Granville-Grossman, 1966; Gregory, 1966; Munro, 1966 *a*) have failed to show any significant difference in the incidence of early parent death in patients and controls. It is noteworthy that those studies with positive findings tend to suggest that early childhood is the most critical period for loss to occur. Significant findings have been reported in the following studies: Norton (1952), father death prior to age 10; Barry and Lindemann (1960), mother death prior to age 5; Archibald *et al.* (1962), death of either parent prior to age 13, and Hilgard and Newman (1963) mother death prior to age 6 and father death prior to age 12 (this finding was calculated from the original data, as results were presented as mean age at parent death).

It may be argued that information about events during early life is likely to be inaccurate, as the subject depends largely upon what he has been told. He may assume that his father died when he was young when in fact he is illegitimate or his father deserted. Parent suicide is more easily concealed during this period. This argument may also apply to the control subjects, though because of a known familial association between mental illness and desertion or suicide, it would apply more to the patient group.

The two studies of Brown (1961) and Dennehy (1966) have concluded that parent death, particularly father death, occurring between ages 10 and 14, is important in depressives and alcoholics. This runs counter to the argument

Table VI

Mean Age of Parent at Birth for those who Suffered Parent Death before Age 20

	Father				Mother				Total father	Total mother
	Son		Daughter		Son		Daughter			
	n	Mean age	n	Mean age	n	Mean age	n	Mean age		
Patients	35	36·5	41	37·3	21	30·2	32	30·4	36·9	30·4
Controls	29	35·4	32	37·8	19	32·6	27	32·3	36·6	32·4
Differences	1·1		·5		2·4		1·9		·3	2·1

Father: sons	t = ·400	d.f. = 62	p = ·7
daughters	t = ·010	d.f. = 71	p > ·9
Mother: sons	t = ·926	d.f. = 38	p = ·35
daughters	t = ·965	d.f. = 57	p = ·33
Total father	t = ·171	d.f. = 135	p = ·86
Total mother	t = 1·352	d.f. = 97	p = ·18

66

that the early years are the most critical for loss to occur.

A significant relationship between early parent death and age is present only in the control group. It is suggested that this may be due to the excessive incidence of parent death between ages 0 and 19 in the patients aged 20 to 39 compared with the controls with the same age distribution. A possible explanation for this is that in this younger group of patients the effects of recent parent deaths occurring between ages 10 and 19 is combined with that of early parent deaths occurring between ages 0 and 9.

The relationship between early parent death and parental age at birth has been considered by Moran (1968). It is important to establish whether a high incidence of early parent death is merely a reflection of high parental age at birth. Moran has concluded that, though there is a clear relationship between the two factors, neither is completely explanatory of the other and thus both probably operate together. It should be stressed that the mean parental ages at birth quoted in the present study are only for those subjects whose parents have died. That there is little difference between the mean parental ages at birth for patients and controls who have suffered early parent death suggests that any association which might exist between early parent death and mean parental age at birth is the same in both the patient and the control group. This would indicate that the raised incidence of early parent death in the patients is a primary phenomenon and is not secondary to increased parental age at birth. Munro (1966 b) has obtained estimates of the mean parental ages at birth for a sample of the Edinburgh general population, whether or not early parent death has occurred. The age distribution, and therefore the era through which the patients have lived, is comparable with that of the present study. His figure for mean maternal age at birth (30·37) corresponds closely with the mean ages in the present study, suggesting that there is no relationship between mean maternal age at birth and early mother death. His figure for mean paternal age at birth (33·08) is significantly less than those in the present study (36·9 and 36·6)* and suggests that the incidence of early father death, both in the general population and among the patients, is associated with a later age at birth of subject.

During the 0 to 4 age span the difference between patients and controls is as marked for father deaths as it is for mother deaths. It might have been expected that the difference would be most marked for mother deaths, for during early years the child's relationship to the mother is more intimate. However, the eventual effect of early parent death is that from the time of death onwards, the child must survive without that parent though there may be a substitute parent. This finding supports the view that it is not so much the trauma of separation from the parent as the continued absence of the parent throughout childhood which is the important aspect of early parent death.

In the present study the numbers are too small to examine the relationship between early parent death and diagnosis. It is not likely that the incidence is disproportionately high among depressives. This question will be considered further in a separate paper.

Summary

1. A sample of 500 admissions to a Scottish psychiatric hospital has been compared with a sample of similar size matched for age and sex from a local general practice.

2. In the control group a clear relationship exists between age and early parent death, indicating the need for matching for age.

3. The incidence of parent death before age 20 is significantly higher in patients under 40, but not in patients over 40. It is proposed that this may be due to the additional effect of recency in the younger patients.

4. The incidence of parent death before age 10 is significantly higher in the patient group.

* Raw data kindly supplied by Dr. Munro. Comparison between the two control groups = t = 2·6734, d.f. = 215, p = ·007.

During this age-period loss of fathers alone and loss by daughters alone are significant.

5. The most marked difference between patients and controls occurs during the 0 to 4 age span, loss of both fathers and mothers alone and loss by daughters alone being significant.

6. The mean parental ages at birth for patients and controls who have suffered early parent death do not differ significantly, suggesting that parent death, and not parental age at birth, is the primary phenomenon.

ACKNOWLEDGMENTS

I wish to thank Dr. A. C. Tait, Physician Superintendent and formerly Director of Clinical Research at the Crichton Royal Hospital, for advice and criticism; Dr. G. Watt, Langholm, Dumfriesshire, for permission to include his patients in the population survey; Dr. G. Beavans and Mr. D. Hall for statistical guidance; and Dr. J. Baldwin for reading of the final draft.

REFERENCES

1. ARCHIBALD, H. *et al.* (1962). "Bereavement in childhood and adult psychiatric disturbance." *Psychosom. Med.*, **24**, 343–351.

2. BARRY, H., Jr., and LINDEMANN, E. (1960). "Critical ages for maternal bereavement in psychoneurosis." *Ibid.*, **22**, 166–179.

3. BRILL, N., and LISTON, E. (1966). "Parental loss in adults with emotional disorders." *Arch. gen. Psychiat.*, **14**, 307–313.

4. BROWN, F. (1961). "Depression and childhood bereavement." *J. ment. Sci.*, **107**, 754–777.

5. DENNEHY, C. (1966). "Childhood bereavement and psychiatric illness." *Brit. J. Psychiat.*, **112**, 1049–1069.

6. GRANVILLE-GROSSMAN, K. L. (1966). "Early bereavement and schizophrenia." *Ibid.*, **112**, 1027–1034.

7. GREGORY, I. (1966). "Retrospective data concerning childhood loss of a parent." *Arch. gen. Psychiat.*, **15**, 354–361.

8. HILGARD, J., and NEWMAN, M. (1963). "Parental loss by death in childhood as an aetiological factor among schizophrenic and alcoholic patients compared with a non-patient community sample." *J. nerv. ment. Dis.*, **137**, 14–28.

9. MORAN, P. (1968). "Maternal age and parental loss." *Brit. J. Psychiat.*, **114**, 207–214.

10. MUNRO, A. (1966 *a*). "Parental deprivation in depressive patients." *Ibid.*, **112**, 443–457.

11. —— (1966 b). "Some familial and social factors in depressive illness." *Ibid.*, **112**, 443–457.

12. NORTON, A. (1952). "Incidence of neurosis related to maternal age and birth order." *Brit. J. soc. Med.*, **6**, 253–258.

13. PITTS, F., MEYER, J., BROOKS, M., and WINOKUR, G. (1965). "Adult psychiatric illness assessed for parent loss." *Amer. J. Psychiat.*, **121**, Childhood Supplement.

Recent Parent Death and Mental Illness

By JOHN BIRTCHNELL

Reaction to the death of a closely related person is characterized by a period of shocked disbelief, a period of acceptance and suffering, during which time the libidinal attachment to the internalized object is gradually withdrawn, and a prolonged period of readjustment. The first two phases usually last a number of months and correspond to the state of acute grief described by Lindemann (1944), Wretmark (1959) and Parkes (1965). The third phase involves the adjustment to a life without the lost person and in some individuals may persist for a number of years.

Studies of recent bereavement, such as those of Parkes (1964a and b, 1965) have been concerned with patients whose illness has appeared to develop within six months of the death of a relative. The physical or mental symptomatology have been considered as a manifestation of the state of acute grief. The present study is concerned more with the mental state during the third phase of re-adjustment. As far as is known there have been no previous epidemiological studies of this phase.

The aim of this study is to determine whether more than the expected number of psychiatric patients have experienced parental bereavement during a period of years before admission, and therefore whether bereavement has contributed to their illness or their need for admission. As the study is not concerned with the effects of acute grief, patients who were bereaved during the year of admission have been excluded; though some patients admitted early in the year, whose parents died late in the previous year, will inevitably have been included. The incidence of parent death occurring 1 to 5, 6 to 10 and 11 to 20 years before admission has been compared with that occurring over a comparable period in a local population control group.

An important distinction should be drawn between the present study of recent parent death and studies of early parent death. In a study of recent loss the temporal relationship between bereavement and admission is considered. In a study of early loss the age of the subject at the time of bereavement is considered. In young subjects a death can be considered either as 'early' or 'recent'. The minimum age in all comparisons is twenty, thus there is no overlap between the first ten years of life and the ten year period preceding admission.

The following aspects of recent parent death will be considered:

  (i)   the sex of the parent lost
  (ii) the sex of the bereaved
  (iii) the current age of the bereaved
  (iv) the marital status of the bereaved
  (v) the number of years before admission the bereavement occurred
  (vi) the incidence of recent parent death in first and re-admissions
  (vii) recent and early bereavement in the same patient.

METHOD

The design of the study and the composition of the patient group has been given in a previous paper investigating the incidence of early parent death in the same patient and control group (Birtchnell, 1970). In summary, information was obtained from the case records of 500 admissions to the Crichton Royal Hospital, Dumfries, between the years 1959 and 1963. Missing information was obtained by postal questionnaire and visits by mental welfare officers.

All diagnostic groups were included, as were both first admissions and re-admissions. Information about the Dumfriesshire population was obtained by sending a questionnaire similar to the one used for the patient group to 500 subjects matched for age and sex obtained from the age/sex register of a general practitioner in Langholm. Replies were received from 473 subjects, and these have been used as the control group.

As the same groups of patients and controls have been used for both early and recent parent death studies, they are matched for age in 1963: appropriate for early parent death studies, but not for age on admission (which would be appropriate for recent parent death studies). This difficulty has been overcome by calculating the number of deaths that would have been associated with the patient group had it experienced the death rates of the control group. The calculation was carried out using three age-groups (20–39, 40–49, 50–59), each subdivided by the three groupings of the interval of time between parent death and admission (1–5, 6–10, 11–20). For each of the nine groups thus obtained the number of deaths expected was calculated by multiplying the death rate for the controls by the number of patients.

There are two possible ways of expressing incidence. It may be expressed as a percentage of the total known cases, as in the early parent death study, or as a percentage of the number of patients remaining capable of losing the particular parent. In the first method a clear indication of the incidence of recent parent death, as opposed to death occurring at any other time, is presented, but this does not indicate whether those not recorded as having suffered recent parent death have lost the parent earlier in life or still have that parent alive. In the second method, all cases whose parent was known to have died before the year span considered have been subtracted from the denominator. As early parent death has been shown to be excessive in psychiatric patients, the second method is more acceptable and has been used in all calculations. The number of cases for which it is not known whether the parent is dead or alive, and in the case of recent father death, illegitimates, have also been subtracted from the denominator.

Parent death in all cases refers to the natural parent and not to a step-parent or person who has come to be looked upon as a parent. A statement stressing this was made in the questionnaires. When both parents have died during the twenty year period considered, only the most recent death has been counted and used in the calculations. This is because it is considered preferable to measure the number of individuals who have suffered parent death rather than the number of parents who have died. However, in obtaining the appropriate denominators for mother and father deaths all parent deaths must be taken into account, whether or not they were the most recent, to achieve the correct 'at risk' group.

RESULTS

Table I gives the age and sex distribution of the patient and control group, together with the denominators and incidences of parent death occurring during the complete twenty year period. The incidences in the two groups are remarkably similar: 29·2 per cent of the patients compared with 31·5 per cent of the controls have suffered recent mother death and 34·2 per cent of the patients compared with 34·0 per cent of the controls have suffered recent father death. As might be expected, a very clear relationship exists between age and the incidence of recent parent death. For both patients and controls the difference in the incidence of mother and father death in those younger and older than age 40 is highly significant. This is not surprising, as the denominator in these comparisons comprises only those whose parents have yet to die. Table II presents the data from the Dumfriesshire control sample which is used to obtain expected numbers of parent deaths for comparison with the observed numbers of deaths in the patient group. Table III compares the observed and expected numbers of mother and father deaths. It will be seen that there is a close correspondence between the observed and expected numbers for the complete twenty year period before admission. During the most recent five year period, death of either parent is significantly greater than expected, but during the previous five year period it is significantly less than expected. During the period 11–20 years before admission there is no significant difference between the observed and expected number. Though mother and father deaths alone show trends similar to the deaths of either parent, they do not reach significance.

Table IV compares the observed and expected numbers of recent parent deaths in sons and daughters. In the most recent five year period, the observed number of parent deaths for both sons and daughters together is in excess of the expected number, and this excess is significant for daughters alone. In the previous five year period, the expected number is greater for both sexes. In the period 11–20 years before admission, significantly more sons and significantly less daughters suffered parent death.

74

TABLE I

The age and sex distribution of the patient and control group, the numbers in each age group with mother and father known to be alive up to the twenty year period considered, and the incidence of mother and father death for each age group during this period.

Patients

Age on admission	Number in age group			Number with parents known to be alive up to 20 year period		Parent death over 20 year period	
	Men	Women	Total	Mother	Father	Mother	Father
<20	7	5	12	11	9	1 (6·3%)	3 (13·6%)
20–24	25	24	49	48	44	3 (10·3%)	6 (25·0%)
25–29	17	24	41	39	36	4 (20·4%)	9 (31·7%)
30–34	31	22	53	49	41	10 (20·0%)	13 (29·5%)
35–39	38	46	84	70	61	14 (30·5%)	18 (41·7%)
40–44	29	40	69	59	48	18 (35·7%)	20 (42·6%)
45–49	30	45	75	56	47	20 (57·8%)	20 (57·1%)
50–54	35	36	71	45	35	26 (87·5%)	20 (40·0%)
55–59	20	26	46	24	15	21	6
Total	232	268	500	401	336	117 (29·2%)	115 (24·2%)

Controls

Age in 1963	Number in age group			Number with parents known to be alive up to 20 year period		Parent death over 20 year period	
	Men	Women	Total	Mother	Father	Mother	Father
20–24	17	24	41	40	36	2 (5·0%)	9 (25·0%)
25–29	21	17	38	36	34	5 (13·0%)	5 (14·7%)
30–34	27	23	50	48	44	4 (8·3%)	11 (25·0%)
35–39	31	41	72	66	64	18 (27·3%)	23 (35·9%)
40–44	39	39	78	66	56	20 (30·3%)	15 (26·8%)
45–49	21	39	60	45	37	21 (46·7%)	20 (54·1%)
50–54	29	26	55	37	32	22 (59·5%)	16 (50·0%)
55–59	33	46	79	46	32	29 (63·0%)	15 (46·9%)
Total	218	255	473	384	335	121 (31·5%)	114 (34·0%)

Chi square comparison of parent death in patients younger and older than age 40 on admission and control subjects younger and older than 40 in 1963.
Patients: mother death, $\chi^2 = 47\cdot6578$, d.f. = 1, p < ·001; father death $\chi^2 = 14\cdot4456$, d.f. = 1, p < ·001.
Controls: mother death $\chi^2 = 46\cdot0009$, d.f. = 1, p < ·001; father death $\chi^2 = 8\cdot4412$, d.f. = 1, p < ·01.

TABLE II

The Incidence of recent parent death in the Dumfriesshire control sample

The expected numbers of parent deaths have been obtained by applying the percentages in this table to the appropriate patient denominators.

Period considered	Age in 1963	Mother				Father			
		Sons		Daughters		Sons		Daughters	
		Parents known to be alive up to period	Incidence of loss	Parents known to be alive up to period	Incidence of loss	Parents known to be alive up to period	Incidence of loss	Parents known to be alive up to period	Incidence of loss
1959–1963 ..	20–39	82	7 (8·5%)	91	7 (7·7%)	70	8 (11·4%)	72	6 (8·3%)
	40–49	40	7 (17·5%)	43	8 (18·6%)	32	7 (21·9%)	30	6 (20·0%)
	50–59	19	7 (36·8%)	18	4 (22·2%)	15	2 (13·3%)	9	3 (33·3%)
1954–1958 ..	20–39	85	2 (2·4%)	96	5 (5·2%)	77	8 (10·4%)	83	10 (12·1%)
	40–49	43	6 (14·0%)	49	6 (12·2%)	39	6 (15·4%)	34	5 (14·7%)
	50–59	27	9 (33·3%)	25	8 (32·0%)	17	3 (17·7%)	13	2 (15·4%)
1944–1953 ..	20–39	90	5 (5·6%)	100	3 (3·0%)	82	4 (4·9%)	96	12 (12·5%)
	40–49	50	4 (8·0%)	61	10 (16·4%)	44	3 (6·8%)	49	8 (16·3%)
	50–59	40	9 (22·5%)	43	14 (32·6%)	35	12 (34·3%)	29	9 (31·0%)

Table III

Recent parent death in relation to the sex of the parent lost

Number of years before admission	Mother			Father			Either parent	
	Parent known to be alive up to period	Observed	Expected	Parent known to be alive up to period	Observed	Expected	Observed	Expected
1–5	309	54	41·6	235	43	32·0	97	73·6
6–10	341	26	36·0	265	24	34·1	50	70·1
11–20	390	36	42·3	327	45	44·0	81	86·3
Total		116	119·9		112	110·1	228	230·0

Chi square comparison of observed and expected numbers of bereaved patients:

Death of either parent, 1– 5 years before admission, $\chi^2 = 7 \cdot 4379$, d.f. = 1, p < ·01
6–10 years before admission, $\chi^2 = 5 \cdot 7633$, d.f. = 1, p < ·02
11–20 years before admission, $\chi^2 = 0 \cdot 3255$, d.f. = 1, N.S.

Mother death, 1–5 years before admission, $\chi^2 = 3 \cdot 6962$, d.f. = 1, N.S.
Father death, 1–5 years before admission, $\chi^2 = 3 \cdot 7813$, d.f. = 1, N.S.

TABLE IV

Recent parent death in relation to the sex of the bereaved

The expected number is the sum of the expected number of mother deaths and of father deaths, using a different denominator for each

Number of years before admission	Sons		Daughters		Total	
	Observed	Expected	Observed	Expected	Observed	Expected
1–5	44	35·4	53	39·2	97	74·6
6–10	21	30·0	29	39·8	50	69·8
11–20	46	32·9	35	53·6	81	86·5
Total	111	98·3	117	132·6	228	230·9

Chi square comparison of observed and expected numbers of bereaved patients:
Sons, 1–5 years before admission, $\chi^2 = 2 \cdot 0893$, d.f. = 1, N.S.
Daughters, 1–5 years before admission, $\chi^2 = 4 \cdot 8582$, d.f. = 1, $p < \cdot 05$
Sons, 11–20 years before admission, $\chi^2 = 5 \cdot 2161$, d.f. = 1, $p < \cdot 05$
Daughters, 11–20 years before admission, $\chi^2 = 6 \cdot 4545$, d.f. = 1, $p < \cdot 02$

Table V considers mother and father death occurring during the most recent five year period in relation to the age of the patients on admission. In the younger patients (aged 20–39), the number of father deaths is significantly greater than expected, whereas in the older patients (aged 40–59) the number of mother deaths is significantly greater than expected.

Table VI considers parent death by sons and daughters occurring during the same period. For sons aged 20–39 there are slightly less parent deaths than expected. For sons aged 40–59 there are significantly more. The distribution of deaths for daughters is more even.

Table VII presents recent parent death figures for first admissions and re-admissions separately. Though both groups demonstrate the trends discernible in the total patient group the differences between observed and expected numbers are significant only for the first admissions.

Table VIII compares the marital status of the 97 patients who suffered parent death during the most recent five years with that in a group of patients matched for age and sex who had not lost a parent during the complete twenty year period. There are more single women in the recent loss group, but the numbers are small and do not reach significance.

Table IX gives the mean maternal and paternal age at birth for patients and controls who suffered parent death in the most recent five year period. Unfortunately the age of the parent at birth was not known for 27 patients, but there is no reason to suppose that the 70 patients for which it is known are unrepresentative. The mean ages at birth are very similar, and the differences are not significant.

DISCUSSION

The investigation reveals that in Dumfriesshire in 1963 almost half the adults aged between 20 and 59 had suffered the death of a parent during the previous twenty years, and approximately one-third had suffered parent death during the previous ten years. That similar incidences were obtained for the patient group during twenty and ten year periods before admission is support for the reliability of this finding. Within the most recent ten year period there is an important difference between the patient and the control group. In the patient group there are almost twice as many parent deaths in the most recent five year period than in the less recent period.

79

TABLE V

Comparison of mother and father deaths during the most recent five year period in relation to the age of the patients on admission

Age on admission	Mother			Father			Either parent	
	Parent known to be alive up to period	Observed	Expected	Parent known to be alive up to period	Observed	Expected	Observed	Expected
20–39	182	12	14·7	155	24	15·3	36	30·0
40–49	93	22	16·8	58	14	12·1	36	28·9
50–59	34	20	10·1	22	5	4·6	25	14·7
Total		54	41·6		43	32·0	97	73·6

Chi square comparison of observed and expected numbers of bereaved patients:

Mother death, patients aged 20–39, $x^2 = 0.4959$, d.f. = 1, N.S.
patients aged 40–59, $x^2 = 8.4762$, d.f. = 1, $p < .01$
Father death, patients aged 20–39, $x^2 = 4.9471$, d.f. = 1, $p < .05$
patients aged 40–59, $x^2 = 0.3168$, d.f. = 1, N.S.

Table VI

Parent death occurring during the most recent five year period in relation to the sex of the bereaved and to the age of the patients on admission

The expected number is the sum of the expected number of mother deaths and of father deaths, using a different denominator for each

Number of years before admission	Sons		Daughters		Total	
	Observed	Expected	Observed	Expected	Observed	Expected
20–39	15	16·0	21	13·9	36	29·9
40–49	17	13·0	19	17·2	36	30·2
50–59	12	6·5	13	9·2	25	15·7
Total	44	35·5	53	40·3	97	75·8

Chi square comparison of observed and expected numbers of bereaved patients:
Sons aged 20–39, $\chi^2 = 0.0625$, d.f. = 1, N.S.
Sons aged 40–59, $\chi^2 = 4.6282$, d.f. = 1, p<·05
Daughters aged 20–39, $\chi^2 = 3.6266$, d.f. = 1, N.S.
Daughters aged 40–59, $\chi^2 = 1.1875$, d.f. = 1, N.S.

TABLE VII

Recent parent death in first and re-admissions

The expected number is the sum of the expected number of mother deaths and of father deaths, using a different denominator for each

Number of years before admission	First admissions		Re-admissions		Total	
	Observed	Expected	Observed	Expected	Observed	Expected
1–5	57	43·3	40	30·4	97	73·7
6–10	28	41·5	22	28·6	50	70·1
11–20	51	51·2	30	34·2	81	85·4
Total	136	136·0	92	93·2	228	229·2

Chi square comparison of observed and expected numbers of bereaved patients:

First admissions, 1–5 years before admission, $\chi^2 = 4\cdot3346$, d.f. = 1, p < ·05

6–10 years before admission, $\chi^2 = 4\cdot3916$, d.f. = 1, p < ·05

Re-admissions, 1–5 years before admission, $\chi^2 = 3\cdot0316$, d.f. = 1, N.S.

6–10 years before admission, $\chi^2 = 1\cdot5231$, d.f. = 1, N.S.

TABLE VIII

The marital status of patients whose parents died 1–5 years before admission compared with that of a group of patients matched for age and sex whose parents did not die during the 20 year period before admission

Marital status	Parent died 1–5 years before admission			Parent did not die during the 20 year period before admission		
	Men	Women	Total	Men	Women	Total
Unmarried	13	15	28	14	7	21
Married (including widowed, divorced, etc.)	31	38	69	30	46	76
Total	44	53	97	44	53	97

Chi square comparison of the marital state of those who did and did not suffer recent parent death:
$\chi^2 = 1 \cdot 3380$, d.f. = 1, N.S.

TABLE IX

Comparison of the mean parental age at birth in patients and controls who suffered parent death over the most recent five year period

Age of parent at birth was not known for 27 patients

	Father		Mother	
	n.	Mean age	n.	Mean age
Patients .. : : : : : :	33	33·9	37	29·8
Controls : : : :	32	34·0	40	30·0
Differences : : : :		0·9		0·2

Father: t = 0·0463, d.f. = 63. N.S.
Mother: t = 0·1376, d.f. = 75. N.S.

It is probably more reasonable that there should be a deficit in parent deaths during the less recent period than that there should be equal numbers in the patient and control group. During the complete ten year period a certain number of parents could be expected to die. If from this pool of parents a disproportionate number have died during the more recent period, there will be a smaller number likely to have died during the less recent period. Putting it a different way, the patient group has been drawn more from those subjects whose parents have died recently than from those whose parents have not, thus suggesting an aetiological association.

The relationship of recent parent death to age depends to some extent upon the method of presentation. If it is presented as a proportion of all subjects with parents still at risk of dying, there is clearly a very close relationship to age; for subjects over age 40 with parents still alive are very much more likely to lose these parents, almost all of whom must be over age 60, than are subjects under age 40. If it is presented irrespective of whether the parents have died during an earlier period, a clearer impression of the distribution of parent death throughout life is obtained. In this case the relationship of mother and father death to age is different. The incidence of mother deaths starts low and rises steadily with age. That of father deaths reaches a peak when the subjects are aged 35 to 40 and then tails off, for after the age of 40 the larger proportion of fathers has already died. These differences are of course due to the fact that men tend to marry at an older age and to die younger.

From Table III it appears that the sex of the parent lost is not important, the trend noted for the most recent ten year period applies equally to death of mother and to death of father. However, when age on admission is considered, as in Table V, it is seen that a greater than expected number of younger patients have lost fathers and a greater than expected number of older patients have lost mothers. Thus in the patient group the normal tendency to lose fathers at a relatively younger age and mothers at a relatively older age is exaggerated. It is questionable whether this implies that young adults are more sensitive to the death of their fathers and older adults are more sensitive to the death of their mothers. There does not appear to be any adequate reason why this should be so. It is more likely that patients react excessively to the normal tendency for fathers to die early and mothers to die late in the subject's life.

The trends described above are reflected in the figures for both sons and daughters, though they only reach significance in the separate consideration of daughters. Women, therefore, are perhaps more sensitive than men to . the death of a parent. This may be because they are more often involved in the terminal nursing of the deceased parent. Separate consideration of the sex of the parent lost suggests that women are as vulnerable to the loss of fathers as to the loss of mothers. The studies of Wretmark (1959) and Parkes (1964b), though concerned more with the effects of acute grief, also concluded that women are more inclined than men to develop mental illness following bereavement. Within the most recent five year period, when age on admission is taken into account, as in Table VI, it appears that patients over age 40, and particularly male patients, are more vulnerable to loss.

It might be predicted that a more definite relationship would exist between first admission and recent parent death, for among re-admissions there must have been other aetiological factors which led to previous admissions. On the other hand, it could be argued that subjects prone to mental illness would be likely to relapse following the death of a parent. Table VII shows that the differences between observed and expected numbers of deaths are only significant among the first admissions.

The relationship of recent parent death to diagnosis has not been dealt with in the present paper. As certain diagnoses are common in certain age groups, and as recent parent death is also related to age, it would be difficult to say whether a high incidence of recent parent death was related to the age distribution or to

86

the diagnosis. It has been shown (Birtchnell, 1966) that when age is taken into account the diagnostic distribution within the recent parent death group does not differ from the expected. It is likely, therefore, that death of a parent influences hospital admission but not the type of illness. Lindemann (1944) described a variety of manifestations of morbid grief, including delayed or postponed grief in which, because of social pressures and expectations, the subject is unable to express his grief until some considerable delay after the bereavement. Anderson (1949), who studied 100 cases of morbid grief over a prolonged period, observed that 'as the work of mourning proceeds so the clinical picture changes'. He was of the opinion that 'it is among the most severe instances of chronic neurosis that there will be found those who are suffering from the extremities of morbid grief . . .'.

It may be expected that the high incidence of parent death in the period 1–5 years before admission is due to a large number occurring within the most recent year. Year by year breakdown of the deaths demonstrates that in four of the five more recent years patient losses exceed those of the controls, and in four of the five previous years control losses are greater.

Unmarried subjects would be expected to react badly to parent death. Failure to marry may be an indication of a continued dependent relationship to the parent, and the subjects may be living with or close to him and are more likely to have to nurse him during the terminal illness. Furthermore they would have no spouse to offer support during the period of mourning. Comparison of the most recent parent death patients with a group of patients matched for age and sex who have not suffered recent parent death reveals no significant difference in the marital status.

As with early parent death studies, it is important to be sure that any difference observed between patients and controls in respect of recent parent death are not secondary to differences in the mean age of the parents at the birth of the subject. In the early parent death study of the same two groups this was shown not to be the case (Table VI). The mean parental ages at birth given in Table IX are very similar in the two groups and correspond closely with the mean ages at birth of mother (30·37) and father (33·08) for the Edinburgh general population obtained by Munro (1966). It is therefore unlikely that parental age is a significant factor.

To examine the relationship between early and recent parent death would require a very large original sample. As has been already mentioned, the two categories of loss are not mutually exclusive. In the present study seven patients and seven control subjects who lost a parent in the most recent ten year period could also be classified as cases of early parent death. These numbers are comparatively small and do not influence the significance of the findings. Twenty-three patients and twenty control subjects who had lost a parent in the most recent ten year period had suffered the death of the first parent in childhood.

The findings of this investigation support the initial hypothesis that the years following parental bereavement represent a period of adjustment and therefore of relative instability, during which admission to a mental hospital is more likely. It is probable that the internal psychological adjustment to the loss is as important as the external adjustment to altered family circumstances.

Summary

1. A sample of 500 admissions to a Scottish psychiatric hospital was compared with a sample of similar size from a local general practice.

2. A definite relationship between recent parent death and age was demonstrated in both the patient group and the general population.

3. Expected numbers of recent parent deaths, in relation to age and sex, were calculated from the general population group and compared with the observed numbers in the patient group.

4. When the complete 20 year period before

admission was considered, the total number of parent deaths among the psychiatric patients corresponded closely with what would be expected over a comparable period in the general population.

5. Though the number of parent deaths occurring during the most recent ten year period before admission is similar to the expected numbers, a disproportionate and significantly higher number of parent deaths occurred in the patient group during the most recent five years of this period. During the less recent five years there was a significantly smaller number of parent deaths.

6. Within the most recent five year period, a greater than expected number of younger patients were found to have suffered recent father death, and a greater than expected number of older patients were found to have suffered recent mother death.

7. Within the same period parent loss by women was significantly greater than expected.

8. A more definite relationship was found between recent parent death and first admission than re-admission.

9. The marital status of those patients who had suffered recent parent death did not differ significantly from a group, matched for age and sex, who had not.

10. The mean parental ages at birth among patients and controls who suffered recent parent death were found to be similar, suggesting that parent death and not parental age at birth is the primary phenomenon.

ACKNOWLEDGEMENTS

I wish to thank Dr. A. C. Tait, Physician Superinten-dent and formerly Director of Clinical Research at the Crichton Royal Hospital for advice and criticism, Dr. G. Watt, Langholm, Dumfriesshire, for permission to include his patients in the population survey and Dr. J. Baldwin and Mr. D. Hall for statistical guidance.

REFERENCES

ANDERSON, C. (1949). 'Aspects of pathological grief and mourning.' Int. J. Psychoanal., 30, 48–55.
BIRTCHNELL, J. (1966). 'Parent death and mental illness.'

M.D. Thesis. University of Edinburgh.

—— (1970). 'Early parent death and mental illness.' *Brit. J. Psychiat.*, 116, 281–8.

LINDEMANN, E. (1944). 'Symptomatology and management of acute grief.' *Amer. J. Psychiat.*, 101, 141–8.

MUNRO, A. (1966). 'Some familial and social factors in depressive illness.' *Brit. J. Psychiat.*, 112, 443–57.

PARKES, C. M. (1964a). 'Effects of bereavement on physical and mental health—a study of the medical records of widows.' *Brit. med. J.*, ii, 274–9.

—— (1964b). 'Recent bereavement as a cause of mental illness.' *Brit. J. Psychiat.*, 110, 198–204.

—— (1965). 'Bereavement and mental illness *Brit. J. med. Psychol.*, 28, 13–26.

WRETMARK, G. (1959). 'A study in grief reactions.' *Acta psychiat. neurol. Scand.*, Supp. 136. 292.

The interrelationship between social class, early parent death, and mental illness[1]

JOHN BIRTCHNELL

The lack of consistency in the findings of the large number of studies of early bereavement and mental illness is disquieting. It may be due in part to the failure of investigators to take into consideration a variety of family variables which influence either the incidence or the outcome of early parent death. Parental social class can affect both the incidence and the outcome.

INCIDENCE

There is ample evidence that mortality rates vary considerably between social classes. Such evidence is most readily available for more recent times—for example, Stockwell (U.S.A.) (1963), the General Register Office (England and Wales) (1958), and the Registrar-General for Scotland (1956). As the present study is concerned with the early death of parents, the more relevant mortality rates would be for the period 1880 to 1940. Unfortunately, during this period, such rates were presented for males only, by occupational groups, and not by the Registrar General's five social classes used in the present investigation. However, it is evident from the Registrar-

[1]During the first part of the study the author held an M.R.C. Clinical Research Fellowship. Extra grants were also provided by the M.R.C. to finance the patient and general population surveys.

General for Scotland's *Decennial Supplements* 1891–1900 (1905) and 1921–1930 (1935) that there were marked gradients in mortality rates between the professional occupations and various categories of unskilled labourers. In particular this was true for the age period 25 to 44, when these men would have been most likely to have had young children. For example, between 1921 and 1930, the comparative mortality rates for men aged 25 to 44 (on the basis of the rate for all males being 100) was 76 for the professional occupations and 124 for labourers and other unskilled workers. It could be reasonably assumed, therefore, that the parents belonging to the classes with the highest mortality rates are more likely to have died during the childhood of their offspring. Langner and Michael (1963) examined by home interviews 1,660 inhabitants of Midtown Manhatten. They observed that in the low parental socioeconomic status group 15·1% had lost a father by death before the age of 16 and 7·9% had lost a mother. In the high parental socioeconomic status group only 12·6% had lost a father by death and only 4·9% had lost a mother. The death of both parents occurred in 2·3% and 0·4% of the two groups respectively. If, for some reason, the social class distribution of the parents of samples of psychiatric patients and general population controls do not correspond, the incidence of early parent death in the two samples cannot be reliably compared. As parental social class is an indication of the family circumstances and living conditions of early years, its distribution among psychiatric patients may not correspond with that of a general population sample, for the children of parents belonging to certain social classes may be more vulnerable to psychiatric breakdown. There is some evidence that this may be so (Birtchnell, 1971a). A recorded raised incidence of early parent death in a particular psychiatric sample may therefore merely be an association with other aspects of the early environment and may not be the primary aetiological factor.

OUTCOME

The effects of early parent death, in terms of

vulnerability to mental illness in adult life, would probably depend upon the closeness of the relationship to the parent before death, the adequacy of replacement of parent care provided after the event, and the degree of disorganization of the family caused by the bereavement. In some occupational groups parents and children are separated for long periods due either to the nature of the parent's occupation—for example, sailor or fisherman—or to the prevailing educational system of the group—for example, being sent away to preparatory and public school. Children in certain classes may therefore be less affected by the parent's death. Lower social class families are larger (Birtchnell, 1970a), and this, combined with their lower income, may create greater hardship and the need for the institutional care of the children. On the other hand, in the more closely knit lower class communities replacement of parental care may be more readily available from older siblings, other relatives, and neighbours, who live close at hand. However, the internal reorganization of the family may not always be advantageous: the premature assumption of the parental role by older siblings may have deleterious effects on their mental state (Birtchnell, 1971b) and older siblings do not make good parent substitutes (Rosenbaum, 1963).

REVIEW OF PREVIOUS STUDIES

Parent social class is frequently not included in psychiatric histories. This is one reason why it has not been considered by the majority of investigators of early parent death. Some have instead considered the subject's current social class. Pitts, Meyer, Brooks, and Winokur (1965) claimed to have matched patients and controls by socioeconomic status but, in fact, only differentiated between ward and private status. Norton (1952) also claimed to have done so but gave no details of how it was carried out. Munro (1966) showed the current social class distribution of his patient and control samples to be similar. Such procedures are of course quite inappropriate, for, even in the general population, current social class distribution is strikingly different from that of parental social class. Furthermore, the social mobility of psychiatric patients differs to a highly significant extent from that of the general population (Birtchnell, 1971c). Thus if groups of patients and controls are matched by current social class it is unlikely that they will be matched by parental social class.

Gregory has always been aware of the need to take parental social class into account in making comparisons of the incidence of early bereavement. In 1965, in an anterospective study of the effects of early parent death upon delinquency, he made allowance for parental social class in calculating the expected numbers of bereaved subjects. In 1966, in a retrospective study of bereavement, he compared the parental social class distribution of 258 patients who would have been aged 3 to 12 years in 1950 with the social class distribution of married males aged 50 years and over in 1950 obtained by Hollingshead and Redlich (1958). Unfortunately, their study had been carried out in a different region of the United States. Langner and Michael (1963) are the only previous investigators to have considered the possibility that the outcome of early bereavement in terms of vulnerability to adult mental illness may differ between parental socioeconomic groups. They found no association between mental health risk and the early death of a mother in the high parental socioeconomic group but a greatly increased risk among the early mother bereaved subjects in the low group. Surprisingly, parental socioeconomic status did not affect the mental health risk of the early father bereaved subjects.

It is highly probable that early parent death, particularly early father death, has an effect upon the current social class of the bereaved individual. As Dennehy (1966) has pointed out, those whose parents die early may need to forgo further education or professional training in order to leave school and become breadwinners for the family. As a result, they may fall behind their non-bereaved contemporaries in occupational status. Gregory (1965) demonstrated a higher incidence of high school drop-out in those who had been bereaved of a parent of the same sex. This is, of course, another reason why it is inappropriate to match patients and controls by current social class in studies of early bereavement. In so doing one may be cancelling out an effect one may wish to observe.

In the present study a number of relationships between social class and early parent death are examined. (1) Using a general population sample, the incidence of early bereavement in the five parental social class groups is compared, to determine the extent to which parental social class does influence the incidence of mother and father death occurring from age 0 to 9 and 10 to 19. (2) For each parental social class separately, the psychiatric patients and the general population controls are compared in respect of mother and father death occurring during the same two age periods. This obviates the necessity for matching by parental social class and, at the same time, reveals whether the outcome of early bereavement, in terms of vulnerability to later mental illness, varies between parental social classes. As it appears that severely ill patients are the group most affected by early bereavement (Birtchnell, 1970b, 1971c), a separate sub-sample of patients who have received at least one month's inpatient treatment are included in these comparisons. (3) The age of termination of full-time education is compared in early bereaved and non-bereaved patients. (4) The current social class is compared in the early father bereaved and non-bereaved male controls. These final two comparisons should reveal the extent to which bereaved people are required to forgo higher education and, as a result, lag behind their contemporaries in occupational status.

METHOD

The present study is one of a series of investigations based upon the North-Eastern Regional Psychiatric Case Register, which has been in operation in the Department of Mental Health of the University of Aberdeen since January 1963 (Baldwin, Innes, Miller, Sharp, and Dorricott, 1965), and a general population survey carried out by the author in the same region in 1969. One of the aims of these investigations has been to examine systematically those familial factors which might significantly influence the relation-

95

ship between parent death and mental illness.

A very high proprtion of patients referred to the psychiatric services in the north-east of Scotland are interviewed by trained staff, and social and familial data are recorded on standard forms. These forms are stored in numerical sequence in the Mental Health Research Unit. Some of the data are coded and stored on magnetic tape files for use on the university computer. At the time of referral all cases are checked against previous records to avoid duplication. Not all of the information required for the present investigation was included in the magnetic tape store. Additional data were extracted and coded from the original survey forms. In a substantial proportion of cases the patients' records were incomplete. To obtain these missing data a postal survey was carried out and patients who were currently in hospital were interviewed again.

The psychiatric sample comprised 6,795 patients aged 20 or over who were referred to the psychiatric services of the north-eastern region of Scotland during the five-year period 1963–67. Although diagnosis is known, it was not used in the present investigation; instead the 2,407 patients who had received more than one month's inpatient treatment were considered separately, as representing a more severely ill group.

The general population survey was carried out on a systematic random sample of 4,000 subjects aged 20 or over, selected from the lists of seven general practices in the north-eastern region of Scotland. The practices were selected by the General Practice Teaching and Research Unit of the University of Aberdeen as being typical of the region by age and social class distribution. They included four from the city of Aberdeen (2,000 subjects), two from small towns to the north (1,100 subjects), and one from a coastal village to the south (900 subjects). This was in accordance with the knowledge that 50% of the psychiatric referrals were from the city of Aberdeen. The number of subjects over age 20 in each practice was divided by the number required and the calculated proportion of National Health Service envelopes, stored alphabetically, were extracted at appropriate intervals.

Patients on general practitioners' lists were chosen, in preference to a sample from the electoral register, because (1) their age and approximate social class distribution were known and (2) it was felt that a personal appeal by the general practitioner would evoke a better response. Questionnaires were sent, together with a covering letter, signed by the general practitioner, requesting that the completed forms be returned anonymously to him. New questionnaires and reminder letters were sent at intervals of two and four weeks. It was decided to restrict the questions asked to social class of parent and subject, details of upbringing, including parent death, and constitution of sibship. It was felt that more extensive questioning would have reduced the response rate. The questions which permitted classification by social class were: 'What is your occupation? (If you are a married woman, please state only your husband's occupation)' and 'What was your father's occupation during your childhood?' The questions relating to parent death were: 'Is your (natural) mother still alive? If she is not, in what year did she die? How old were you when she died? Is your (natural) father still alive? If he is not, in what year did he die? How old were you when he died?' Replies were received from 3,425 subjects —that is, 85·6%. The responses from the city and the more rural practices were identical. It was not possible to estimate the parental social class or social class distribution of the non-respondents, though the social class distribution of the respondents was in reasonable accord with available census data for north-east Scotland. The age and sex distribution of the final control sample was comparable with that of the patient sample.

Parent death was in all cases that of the natural parent and not of a step-parent, foster parent, or person who had come to be looked upon as a parent. As this is a study of bereaved individuals, and not of parents lost, only the first parent to die in childhood has been counted. If both parents died in the same year, however, both the mother and the father death has been counted separately. Information about early father death was not known for $8·0\%$ of patients and 4·5% of controls. Information about early mother death was not known for 3·1% of patients and 1·7% of controls. These percentages include illegitimates (4·2% of patients and probably a smaller percentage of controls) and those brought up in institutions or foster homes (approximately 2% of patients and 1% of controls). These cases were excluded from the denominators in all calculations. As the expectation of life (of parents) varies between urban and rural areas (Glass, 1964), the incidence of early parent death may also do so. There is no way of telling whether the parents of the patients and the controls lived in comparable geographical areas, for the two groups may differ in the extent to which they migrate between urban and rural areas. It is to be hoped that this variable has been allowed for by ensuring that the groups were comparable in their current area of residence.

The social class too was that of the natural parents and the classification was based upon his usual occupation. Though it is probable that the social class of a replacement parent is similar to that of the lost parent, it was decided to exclude from the analysis all cases for whom the natural parent's social class was not known. Parental social class was not known for 7·4% of the patients (7·3% of the inpatient sub-sample) and 5·2% of the controls. For a further 4·7% of the patients (4·4% of the inpatient sub-sample) and 2·2% of the controls only the social class of a parent substitute was known. As parental social class is determined by the occupation of the father, it is more likely to be unknown in the father-bereaved patients and controls. Separate analysis of the parental social class unknown group confirms this but also demonstrates that the patient and control groups were equally affected—that is, the incidence of early parent death differed to the same extent as in the total patient and control samples. Thus exclusions of these subjects should not seriously affect the comparisons. Information about the social class of the (male) subject was not known for 0·5% of the patients and 9·3% of the controls; this low percentage for the patients was due to the recording of parental social class as an index of their own social class in the small proportion of

98

cases for whom it was not known. As this was part of the original computer search programme, it could not be avoided for the present study. In fact, it will have the effect of improving slightly the current social class distribution of the patients for they are likely to have fared worse than their parents. The control subjects for whom social class was not known were mainly those whose occupations were inadequately described. It is probable that they included subjects from a variety of social classes.

Because of the difficulty of assigning women to appropriate social classes, only the men were included in comparisons by current social class. The General Register Office *Classification of Occupations* (1960) was used for the social class grouping of both parents and subjects. The social class of patients and of their parents, coded according to the Registrar General's classification, was pre-existent in the Case Register. It was necessary therefore to classify the control sample in identical fashion. It may be argued that the 1960 Classification is not altogether suitable for grading parental social class. Such imprecision as may arise, however, is likely to apply equally to the patient and control samples. The age of termination of full-time education was known only for the patients, but was known for both men and women.

Because of the variation in types of occupation, social class distribution varies from one part of the country to another and also between rural and urban areas. Again, therefore, it is important that the patient and control samples were derived from comparable geographical locations.

RESULTS

DOES PARENTAL SOCIAL CLASS AFFECT THE INCIDENCE OF EARLY PARENT DEATH?

As there may be significant associations between mental illness and both parental social class and early parent death, it is preferable to use only the control data to determine the extent to which parental social class affects the incidence of early parent death. The Figure presents, for the control sample only, the incidence of the death of mother and of father before the age of 10 and

99

of death of either parent during this period for parental social classes I and II combined, III, IV, and V. Because mortality rates tend to be higher in lower social classes, it is probable that the incidence of early parent death would be higher as well. Though this was the case, the differences between the classes were small, the incidence of early father death rising from 3·9% in classes I and II to 6·7% in class V and that of early mother death rising from 2·7% in classes I and II to 3·3% in class V. Furthermore, the observed distribution did not differ significantly from an 'expected' even one. This is not to say,

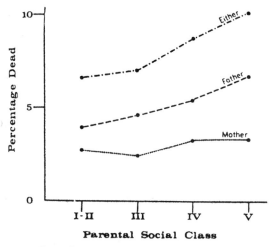

FIGURE *Control sample only: the incidence of the death of a parent before the subject was aged 10 years by parental social class.*

however, that these differences would not have an effect upon comparisons between samples, in respect of early parent death, should there be discrepancies in the parental social class distribution of the samples. The incidence of parent death occurring from the age of 10 to 19 was practically the same in all social classes.

DOES PARENTAL SOCIAL CLASS AFFECT THE OUTCOME OF EARLY PARENT DEATH?

In order to determine the extent to which parental social class affects the outcome of early parent death (in terms of vulnerability to adult mental

TABLE 1

PARENTAL SOCIAL CLASS I AND II: INCIDENCE OF EARLY PARENT DEATH, EXPRESSED AS PERCENTAGE OF KNOWN CASES, FOR CONTROLS, TOTAL PATIENT GROUP, AND SUB-SAMPLE OF PATIENTS WHO RECEIVED AT LEAST ONE MONTH'S INPATIENT TREATMENT

Age at death of parent (yr.)	Father			Mother			Either parent		
	Controls	Allpatients	Inpatients	Controls	Allpatients	Inpatients	Controls	Allpatients	Inpatients
0 to 9	3·9	4·3	4·0	2·7	2·7	3·4	6·6	7·1	7·5
10 to 19	7·3	9·7	12·9	4·7	4·3	5·4	12·1	14·3	18·4
Total early parent death	11·2	14·0	16·9	7·4	7·0	8·8	18·7	21·4	25·9
Not known (actual numbers)	13	38	22	7	30	21	13	45	26
Total	709	1,604	602	709	1,604	602	709	1,604	602

Father died age 10 to 19: father known not to have died before age 20, controls: inpatients, $\chi^2 = 11\cdot7045$, d.f. $= 1$, P $< 0\cdot001$. Other differences are not statistically significant.

TABLE 2

PARENTAL SOCIAL CLASS III: INCIDENCE OF EARLY PARENT DEATH EXPRESSED AS PERCENTAGE OF KNOWN CASES, FOR CONTROLS, TOTAL PATIENT GROUP, AND SUB-SAMPLE OF PATIENTS WHO RECEIVED AT LEAST ONE MONTH'S INPATIENT TREATMENT

Age at death of parent (yr.)	Father			Mother			Either parent		
	Controls	Allpatients	Inpatients	Controls	Allpatients	Inpatients	Controls	Allpatients	Inpatients
0 to 9	4·6	5·4	6·0	2·4	3·6	3·8	7·0	9·1	9·9
10 to 19	8·0	7·0	5·8	3·8	4·9	6·5	11·8	12·1	12·4
Total early parent death	12·6	12·4	11·8	6·2	8·5	10·3	18·8	21·2	22·3
Not known (actual numbers)	23	48	21	12	27	13	24	57	23
Total	1,266	2,115	719	1,266	2,115	719	1,266	2,115	719

Mother died age 0 to 19: mother known not to have died before age 20, controls: inpatients, $\chi^2 = 12\cdot1969$, d.f. $= 1$, P $< 0\cdot001$.
Mother died age 10 to 19: mother known not to have died before age 20, controls: inpatients, $\chi^2 = 7\cdot7771$, d.f. $= 1$, P $< 0\cdot01$.
Other differences are not statistically significant.

illness), the incidence of early parent death in the controls, the total patient sample and a sub-sample of patients who received at least one month's inpatient treatment, was considered separately for parental social classes 1 and II combined (Table 1), class III (Table 2), IV (Table 3), and V (Table 4). It has been previously shown (Birtchnell, 1971c) that the incidence of early parent death tends to be higher in the inpatient sub-sample than in the total patient group. In almost all of the following comparisons the incidence recorded for the total patient sample fell somewhere between that of the inpatient sub-sample and that of the controls.

In parental social classes I and II the total incidence of early parent death was significantly higher in the inpatient sub-sample than in the controls. This was due almost entirely to a significantly higher incidence of early father death ($P<0.001$). This occurred predominantly in the 10 to 19 years age period. In parental social class III the incidence of early father death was slightly lower in the two patient samples than in the controls, but that of early mother death was significantly higher in the inpatient sub-sample ($P<0.001$). This was evident in both age periods but was more pronounced in the 10 to 19 year old one ($P<0.01$). In parental social class IV loss of either parent before the age of 10 appeared to be the most important differentiating factor and the incidence of such loss was significantly higher in the inpatient subsample ($P<0.01$). The difference was due as much to early mother death as to early father death. In parental social class V there were no significant differences between the patients and the controls and in some instances the incidence of early parent death was lower in the patient samples than in the controls.

DOES EARLY PARENT DEATH AFFECT THE AGE OF TERMINATING FULL-TIME EDUCATION

Unfortunately, the age of terminating education was known only for the patient sample. As it is unlikely that age of termination of education is related to adult mental illness it is reasonable to use the patient data to answer the question. Table 5 presents the percentage distribution, by age at termination of full-time education, for

TABLE 3

PARENTAL SOCIAL CLASS IV: INCIDENCE OF EARLY PARENT DEATH EXPRESSED AS PERCENTAGE OF KNOWN CASES, FOR CONTROLS, TOTAL PATIENT GROUP, AND A SUB-SAMPLE OF PATIENTS WHO RECEIVED AT LEAST ONE MONTH'S INPATIENT TREATMENT

Age at death of parent (yr.)	Father			Mother			Either parent		
	Controls	All patients	Inpatients	Controls	All patients	Inpatients	Controls	All patients	Inpatients
0 to 9	5·4	6·4	7·7	3·2	3·7	4·5	8·7	10·2	12·3
10 to 19	7·4	7·8	7·1	5·1	4·7	4·2	12·6	12·6	11·4
Total early parent death	12·8	14·2	14·8	8·3	8·4	8·7	21·3	22·8	23·7
Not known (actual numbers)	23	41	23	17	31	16	24	49	24
Total	896	1,623	594	896	1,623	594	896	1,623	594

Either parent died age 0 to 9: parents known not to have died before age 20, controls: inpatients, $\chi^2 = 7·08.34$. d.f. = 1, P < 0·01. Other differences are not statistically significant.

TABLE 4

PARENTAL SOCIAL CLASS V: INCIDENCE OF EARLY PARENT DEATH EXPRESSED AS PERCENTAGE OF KNOWN CASES, FOR CONTROLS, TOTAL PATIENT GROUP, AND A SUB-SAMPLE OF PATIENTS WHO RECEIVED AT LEAST ONE MONTH'S INPATIENT TREATMENT

Age at death of parent (yr.)	Father			Mother			Either parent		
	Controls	All patients	Inpatients	Controls	All patients	Inpatients	Controls	All patients	Inpatients
0 to 9	6·7	4·9	3·9	3·3	2·7	2·4	10·1	7·6	6·3
10 to 19	9·1	9·3	7·5	3·7	4·9	5·8	12·8	14·4	13·4
Total early parent death	15·8	14·2	11·4	7·0	7·6	8·2	22·9	22·0	19·7
Not known (actual numbers)	4	14	6	2	5	3	5	12	6
Total	302	631	211	302	631	211	302	631	211

None of the differences in this Table is statistically significant.

those patients who were bereaved of either parent before the age of 15 and for those who were known not to have been early bereaved. It would appear that proportionally more of the early bereaved than those who were not early bereaved left school before they were 15. In fact, the difference between the distributions is highly significant for both men and women. It must be remembered, however, that there has been a tendency during this century for people to remain in education progressively longer. Consequently there is a marked relationship between decade of birth and age of terminating education. For example, of those born in 1910–19, 69·4% left school before the age of 15 and only 6·4% continued in education beyond the age of 19; whereas of those born in 1940–49, only 2·1% left school before the age of 15 and 21·2% continued in education beyond the age of 19. When the expected termination of education distribution, based upon decade of birth, was calculated for the early bereaved, it was clear that the difference between the early bereaved and non-bereaved was almost entirely attributable to the fact that the early bereaved were a somewhat older group. The observed and expected termination of education distributions of the early bereaved were not significantly different.

DOES EARLY PARENT DEATH AFFECT CURRENT SOCIAL CLASS?

Because of the known association between current social class and mental illness (Birtchnell, 1971a) it is preferable to use the control data to test the association between early parent death and current social class. As early mother death was found not to affect current social class, Table 6 presents the findings only for early father death. It shows the current social class for the male controls whose fathers died when they themselves were aged 0 to 9 years and 10 to 19 years and for those who were known not to have lost their fathers in childhood. Of those whose fathers died when they were aged 0 to 9 there was a slight deficit in social classes I and II and a slight excess in social class V, compared with the social class distribution of the non-bereaved males. These differences were not statistically significant. Of

TABLE 5

PERCENTAGE DISTRIBUTION, BY AGE AT TERMINATION OF FULL-TIME EDUCATION, OF EARLY BEREAVED AND NOT EARLY BEREAVED PATIENTS*

	Age at termination of full-time education					Not known (actual numbers)	Total
	Under 14	14	15	16 to 19	Over 19		
Parent died before patient was 15							
Men	9·7 (7·1)	51·0 (49·3)	16·4 (21·6)	12·7 (12·7)	10·2 (9·4)	3	405
Women	7·3 (6·2)	50·7 (51·2)	20·9 (21·3)	15·5 (14·5)	5·4 (6·8)	2	613
Not known (actual numbers)							
Men	22	122	70	15	12	3	244
Women	39	149	85	29	13	3	318
Not early bereaved (0 to 19)							
Men	5·8	44·4	26·0	12·8	11·1	13	2,030
Women	4·8	45·0	26·0	15·6	8·6	18	2,774
Total							
Men	189	1,298	698	365	292	19	2,861
Women	224	1,819	977	589	301	24	3,934

* The expected distribution based upon decade of birth is given in parentheses.

TABLE 6

CURRENT SOCIAL CLASS DISTRIBUTION OF EARLY FATHER BEREAVED AND NOT EARLY FATHER BEREAVED MALE CONTROLS

Age at death of father (yr.)	Social class					
	I and II	III	IV	V	Not known	Total
0 to 9	19 (24·7%)	36 (46·8%)	13 (16·9%)	9 (11·7%)	10	87
10 to 19	17 (19·5%)	35 (40·2%)	25 (28·7%)	10 (11·4%)	11	98
Illegitimate or otherwise not known	10	16	13	10	12	61
Not early father bereaved	311 (27·4%)	544 (47·9%)	189 (16·6%)	92 (8·1%)	105	1,241
Total	357	631	240	121	138	1,487

Chi-square comparison, bereaved age 0 to 9: not early bereaved, $\chi^2 = 1\cdot3315$, d.f. $= 3$, NS.
Chi-square comparison, bereaved age 10 to 19: not early bereaved, $\chi^2 = 10\cdot7283$, d.f. $= 3$, P $< 0\cdot02$.

106

those whose fathers died when they were aged 10 to 19 there was a marked deficiency in social classes I, II, and III, a marked excess in class IV, and a slight excess in class V, compared with the distribution of the non-bereaved males. These differences were statistically significant ($P < 0.02$).

It was previously shown (Birtchnell, 1971a) that current social class distribution varies with decade of birth. To ascertain whether the differences in social class distribution between the early bereaved and non-bereaved might be due to the fact that the early bereaved were older, expected social class distributions based upon decade of birth were calculated. The expected distribution of the non-bereaved corresponded closely with the observed one. That of the group whose fathers died when they were aged 10 to 19 was similar to that of the non-bereaved, but quite different from the observed distribution. This demonstrated clearly that the differences in current social class distributions were not due to the age structure of the two groups.

DISCUSSION

Despite the fact that mortality rates are known to vary considerably with social class, the relationship found in the present study between the incidence of early parent death and parental social class was less marked than might have been expected. Though slight, it was in the anticipated direction, the incidence of parent death occurring before age 10 rising from 6.6% in classes I and II to 10.1% in class V. There was, however, no relationship between parent death occurring from the age of 10 to 19 years and parental social class, the incidence in classes I and II, III, IV, and V being 12.1, 11.8, 12.6, and 12.8% respectively. Langner and Michael (1963), in Midtown Manhatten, considered the relationship between parent death occurring before age 16 and parental socioeconomic status. They found the range to be of a similar order: falling from the highest to the lowest social status by 2.5% for father's death and 3.0% for mother's death. The findings indicate that parental social class does influence the incidence of early parent death to an extent which may affect comparative studies. The extent

107

of this influence is likely to vary from one year to another and from one geographical location to another. It would be wise as a preliminary precaution in studies of early bereavement to check its effect.

With regard to the effects of parental social class on the outcome of early parent death, the present study did not replicate the findings of Langner and Michael (1963). They found that in families of low socioeconomic status the mental health risk associated with the early death of a mother (before the age of 16) was much greater than that associated with having an intact nuclear family. In families of high socioeconomic status there was virtually no difference in the mental health risk of mother bereaved and non-bereaved subjects. In no socioeconomic group was the early death of a father associated with an increased mental health risk. There were of course important methodological differences between the two studies. Langner and Michael conducted home interviews on a community sample. In approximately a quarter of the sample mental illness similar to that observed in a psychiatric clinic or hospital was noted to be present. In the present study a psychiatrically ill sample was compared with a general population one. Over a third of the psychiatric sample had received at least one month's inpatient treatment. It is probable that the psychiatric patients in the present study were more seriously ill than those detected by Langner and Michael.

The findings of the present study, though unexpected, may be explained in the following manner. The lack of any association between early mother death and increased vulnerability to mental illness in social classes I and II may be due to the fact that widowers in these classes are more able to afford nannies or housekeepers or are better able to arrange for their children to go to boarding school. Death of father in classes I and II may, on the other hand, have quite serious consequences, particularly in terms of financial loss and loss in social status. In social class III, where there is a highly significant association between mother bereavement occurring before the age of 20 and adult mental illness, there are likely to be more difficulties in securing adequate

108

replacement of the lost mother. Social class IV is most representative of the patient group as a whole in showing an excessive loss of either parent before the age of 10 in the patient group. The absence of any association between early bereavement and mental illness in social class V may be due to the fact that, within the more closely knit, Scottish lower social class communities, adequate replacement of parental care is available from siblings, other relatives, and neighbours.

The study provides little support for the prediction that the early death of a parent may result in early termination of education. Though the early bereaved patients left school appreciably earlier than the non-bereaved, this finding was largely accounted for by the fact that the early bereaved were older. When allowance was made for the age difference between the early bereaved and the non-bereaved, there remained a slight tendency for the early bereaved to leave school earlier than would be expected. This small difference can probably be explained by the two facts that children from the lower social classes have always left school earlier than those from the higher classes and the incidence of early bereavement is higher among children from lower social class families. This conclusion is not in agreement with the observation of Gregory (1965) in America, that the incidence of high-school drop-out was increased by bereavement of the parent of the same sex. Gregory had no need to make adjustment for age, for as his was an anterospective study, the subjects were of similar age distribution.

The study does, however, provide some evidence that early parent death has an effect upon occupational status in later life. The difference in social class distribution between the early bereaved and non-bereaved controls proved not to be related to the difference in age of the two groups and therefore indicates that the early bereaved tended not to reach such high social class as the non-bereaved. It might be concluded, therefore, that, though there is only a suggestion that the early bereaved tend to leave school earlier than they should, it is highly probable that they decline occupations requiring extensive training with good prospects, in preference to those which bring early financial reward.

This study forms part of a large investigation of a variety of familial factors in mental illness involving the North-Eastern Regional Psychiatric Case Register (Scotland) and a local population control group. I am indebted to Dr. John Baldwin for his assistance in planning and carrying this out and to Mr. John Evans for organizing the Aberdeen computer search. I would like to thank Dr. C. C. Spicer, Director of the M.R.C. Computer Unit, for devising a programme for the analysis of the data and Miss Valerie Coulson for carrying out the analysis. I am most grateful to Professor Ian Richardson of the Aberdeen General Practice Teaching and Research Unit and the general practitioners of the North-East of Scotland for their generous cooperation in the general population survey. I would like also to thank the technical and clerical staff of the Mental Health Research Unit, Aberdeen, and a number of temporary research assistants for their help in the tedious collection and preparation of the data. Finally, I should like to express my appreciation of the encouragement and advice of Dr. Peter Sainsbury and other members of the M.R.C. Clinical Psychiatry Unit in Chichester.

REFERENCES

Baldwin, J. A., Innes, G., Millar, W. M., Sharp, G. A., and Dorricott, N. (1965). A psychiatric case register in North-East Scotland. *British Journal of Preventive and Social Medicine*, **19**, 38–42.

Birtchnell, J. (1970a). Sibship size and mental illness. *British Journal of Psychiatry*, **117**, 303–308.

Birtchnell, J. (1970b). Depression in relation to early and recent parent death. *British Journal of Psychiatry*, **116**, 299–306.

Birtchnell, J. (1971a). Social class, parental social class, and social mobility in psychiatric patients and general population controls. *Psychological Medicine*, **1**, 209–221.

Birtchnell, J. (1971b). Early parent death in relation to sibship size and composition in psychiatric patients and general population controls. *Acta Psychiatrica Scandinavica*, **47**, 250–270.

Birtchnell, J. (1971c). Case-register study of bereavement. *Proceedings of the Royal Society of Medicine*, **64**, 279–282.

Dennehy, C. M. (1966). Childhood bereavement and psychiatric illness. *British Journal of Psychiatry*, **112**, 1049–1069.

General Register Office (*1958*). *Decennial Supplement, England and Wales, 1951. Occupational Mortality. Part 2, Volume 2. Tables.* HMSO: London.

Glass, D. V. (1964). Some indicators of differences between urban and rural mortality in England and Wales and Scotland. *Population Studies*, **17**, 263–267.

Gregory, I. (1965). Anterospective data following childhood loss of a parent. I. Delinquency and high school dropout. *Archives of General Psychiatry*, **13**, 99–109.

Gregory, I. (1966). Retrospective data concerning childhood loss of a parent. I. Actuarial estimates vs recorded frequencies of orphanhood. *Archives of General Psychiatry*, **15**, 354–361.

Hollingshead, A. B., and Redlich, F. C. (1958). *Social Class and Mental Illness.* Wiley: New York.

Munro, A. (1966). Parental deprivation in depressive patients. *British Journal of Psychiatry,* **112,** 443–457.

Norton, A. (1952). Incidence of neurosis related to maternal age and birth order. *British Journal of Social Medicine,* **6,** 253–258.

Pitts, F. N., jr., Meyer, J., Brooks, M., and Winokur, G. (1965). Adult psychiatric illness assessed for childhood parental loss, and psychiatric illness in family members— a study of 748 patients and 250 controls. *American Journal of Psychiatry,* **121,** Suppl. No. 12, i–x.

Registrar-General for Scotland (1905) *Annual Report, 1902. Decennial Supplement 1891–1900.* HMSO: Edinburgh.

Registrar-General for Scotland (1934) *Annual Report, 1902. Decennial Supplement 1921–1930.* HMSO: Edinburgh.

Registrar-General for Scotland (1956). *Annual Report 1955, Appendix for Occupational Mortality.* HMSO: Edinburgh.

Rosenbaum, M. (1963). Psychological effects on the child raised by an older sibling. *American Journal of Orthopsychiatry,* **33,** 515–520.

Stockwell, E. G. (1963). A critical examination of the relationship between socioeconomic status and mortality. *American Journal of Public Health.* **53,** 956–964.

EARLY PARENT DEATH, IN RELATION TO SIZE AND CONSTITUTION OF SIBSHIP, IN PSYCHIATRIC PATIENTS AND GENERAL POPULATION CONTROLS

J. Birtchnell

The inconsistencies in the findings of the now considerable number of studies of early parent death are both disconcerting and disheartening. Admittedly, as *Gregory* (1958) has so ably pointed out, most of the earlier studies were methodologically defective. The reliability of parent death studies depends to a large extent upon the control groups used, and the inappropriateness of many of these has been discussed by *Gregory* (1966) and *Dennehy* (1966). There is, furthermore, a wide range of familial variables which may influence the outcome of early bereavement which to date have not been taken into account.

The question of parent replacement has been referred to by a number of investigators, e. g. *Brown* (1966) and *Munro* (1969); and *Anna Freud* (1960) has stated "We have always considered the interval between loss of contact with the mother and attachment to a substitute mother as the period most productive of pathology, especially if this interval is prolonged, either for external reasons (lack of suitable substitute mother) or for internal reasons (inability to transfer cathexis). ... The longer the interval lasts, the more difficult will it be to reverse these pathological developments". As *Fast & Cain* (1966) described, the inability of the substitute parent to accept cathexis and the inability of the remaining parent to transfer his or her cathexis to the new parent are further complicating factors. There is abundant anecdotal evidence of discord between children and their stepparents and this may be due largely to the constant unfavourable comparisons which the child and the remaining parent inevitably will draw between the stepparent and the much loved, still unrelinquished dead parent. *Kaufman, Peck & Tagiuri* (1954) and *Messer* (1969) have demonstrated an increased incidence of incestuous attitudes and relationships between children and their stepparents due to a diminution of the incest taboo. *Cain & Cain* (1962) have shown that there may be emotional difficulties if children are adopted in order to replace one which had previously been lost. Thus parent replacement may be as productive of pathology as is the original loss. The incidence and type of parent substitution in early bereaved psychiatric patients and similarly affected general population controls has been presented elsewhere (*Birtchnell* (1971)).

In the present study the sibships of the same two bereaved groups will be considered. Irrespective of whether a substitute parent has been acquired, it is highly likely that child/parent relationships will become established among the children of a dead parent. The older children, particularly those of the same sex as the lost parent, will come to be looked upon as parent substitutes and will be expected by the remaining parent to help with the care of the younger ones. They may be turned to for solace by the bereaved parent and many become treated almost as spouse. "When bereaved of the adult who offered important emotional satisfactions both parent and child are frequently tempted to turn to one another for substitute gratification" (*Fast & Cain* (1963)). As in the case of stepparents, the relationships between bereaved older and younger siblings may be far from harmonious. The older child may abuse his newly gained power and his former sibling rivalry may become transformed into a sadism untempered by the more naturally acquired parental tenderness (*Rosenbaum* (1963)). The younger one may feel resentment towards the favoured older sibling and may be envious of the oedipal relationship to the remaining parent. *Fast & Cain* (1963) described two mother-bereaved sisters who developed intense oedipal rivalry for their father.

There have been many reports by child psychiatrists of the immediate effects of parent death on children and adolescents. It is a matter for speculation how much these observed reactions are likely to affect subsequent development. *Arthur & Kemme* (1964) studied 34 children who lost a parent of the opposite sex and 49 who lost one of the same sex. They considered that loss of the opposite sexed parent is associated with denial of the loss and sustained fantasy relationships due to a reluctance to relinquish their oedipal attachment; and loss of the same sexed parent is associated with guilt and a need for self-punishment due to the realization of their fantasy to be rid of their oedipal rivals.

It is not easy to predict whether children from large or small sibships are likely to be most affected by early bereavement. One could argue that only children or those from small sibships may have been over-valued or over-indulged by their parents and may therefore suffer more from their loss. Furthermore they have no or fewer siblings to turn to for support. On the other hand, it would be easier to arrange for the care of a small number of siblings, and it may be that the subsequent discord among the bereaved members of a large family may in itself be a damaging factor.

113

The aims of the present investigation are (1) to compare briefly the incidence of early bereavement in a sample of 2,407 psychiatric patients who have received at least one month's in-patient treatment and 3,425 general population controls, (2) to compare the early bereaved psychiatric in-patients and early bereaved controls in respect of size of sibship, presence of older siblings, and presence of younger siblings, and (3) to ensure that the differences which may be observed in the sibships of bereaved in-patients and controls are not also apparent in similar patients and controls who are not early bereaved.

MATERIALS AND METHOD

The source of the psychiatric sample was the North-Eastern Regional Psychiatric Case Register (Scotland) which has been in operation in the Department of Mental Health of the University of Aberdeen since January 1963 (*Baldwin, Innes, Millar, Sharp* & *Dorricott* (1965)). A very high proportion of patients referred to the regional psychiatric services are interviewed by trained staff and social and family data are recorded on standard forms. These forms are stored in numerical sequence in the Mental Health Research Unit. Some of the data are coded and stored on magnetic tape files for use on the University computer. At the time of referral all cases are checked against previous records to avoid duplication. Not all of the detailed information required for the present investigation was included in the magnetic tape store. A programme was written which retrieved as much information as possible in a form most convenient for the analyses envisaged. Data for each patient were represented by a sequence of eighty digits, and spaces were left in the print-out when the required information was not available from the computer. Additional codes were devised and the extra data needed were extracted and coded from the original survey forms. In a substantial proportion of cases, partly because of deficiencies in the design of the early forms used by the interviewers, the patients' records were incomplete. To obtain these missing data, a postal survey, using a detailed three-page questionnaire, was carried out and patients who were currently in hospital were re-interviewed. The extra information obtained was inserted by hand in the appropriate spaces of the computer print-out. This considerably augmented data store was subsequently transferred to the MRC Computer in London for analysis.

The original psychiatric sample comprised 6,795 patients aged 20 or over who were referred to the psychiatric services in the North-Eastern region during the five-year period 1963–67. Although diagnosis is known, it was not used in the present study; instead duration of in-patient treatment has

114

been used as an indication of the severity of the illness. The majority of long-stay in-patients have, to date, not been interviewed and could not therefore be included in the sample. There were, however, 2,407 patients (35.4 %) who had spent more than one month in hospital during the period of three months following contact; and as these might be considered to be the most severely ill, only they have been used in all the present comparisons.

The source of the general population control group was a systematic random sample of subjects aged 20 or over selected from the lists of seven general practices in the North-Eastern Region of Scotland. Four of these practices were in the city of Aberdeen, two were in small towns to the north, and one was in a coastal village to the south. A postal survey was carried out using a questionnaire similar to that used for the psychiatric patients. This was sent together with a covering letter to 4,000 subjects, with reminder letters at intervals of two and four weeks. Replies were received from 3,425 of them, i. e. 85.6 % and these were used as the control group.

Of these, 43.4 % were men, which compares with 42.1 % of the total patient group and 40.6 % of the in-patient subsample.

Though the year of birth distribution in the original patient and control groups corresponded closely, the in-patient subsample is a significantly older group than the control sample (Table 1). This should not affect the relia-bility of the study because (1) it was shown in a previous study (*Birtchnell* (1969)) that in Scotland, at the present time, there is no definite relation-ship between age and the incidence of parent death occurring before age ten, and (2) as an added safeguard the sibship sizes and compositions of the non-bereaved in-patients and controls will be compared with those of the bereaved ones, who have a similar age difference.

Table 1. *Year of birth and sex distribution of in-patient subsample and control group*

		1930–49	1910–29	Before 1910	Not known	Total
Men	In-patients	256 (26.2 %)	408 (41.8 %)	313 (32.0 %)	0	977
	Controls	524 (35.2 %)	608 (40.9 %)	346 (23.3 %)	9	1487
Women	In-patients	315 (22.0 %)	534 (37.3 %)	581 (40.6 %)	0	1430
	Controls	751 (38.8 %)	747 (38.5 %)	436 (22.5 %)	4	1938

2×3 chi-square comparison, patients: controls.
Men $= 32.2051$; d. f. $= 2$, p $< .001$.
Women $= 162.5556$; d. f. $= 2$, p $< .001$.

Presentation of parent death data

Parent death was in all cases intended to be that of the natural parent and not that of a stepparent, foster parent, or person who had come to be looked upon as a parent. Details about parents and substitute parents are listed separately in the case register survey forms and a statement stressing the distinction was made in both the psychiatric patient and general population questionnaires. Because it is the stress of bereavement which is being considered, it is preferable to measure the number of individuals who have experienced parent death rather than the number of parents who have died. Thus when two parents had died during the period of childhood considered, only the first parent to die was included in the calculations. Care has been taken to differentiate, as far as possible, between parent death and other forms of parental absence in childhood. Information about events during early life is likely to be inaccurate, as the subject depends largely upon what he has been told. He may assume that his father died when he was young when in fact he is illegitimate or his father deserted. On the patient survey forms, space is allotted for both death and other forms of separation, and illegitimacy may be detected by comparing maiden name of mother with patient's surname at birth, both of which are routinely recorded. On the questionnaires and in the postal surveys, subjects were asked specifically by whom they were brought up and the period of care of each parent figure.

The sibship of the bereaved subjects

As, in this study, siblings are considered as significant members of the familial environment, miscarriage, still-births, and siblings living only a short time have been excluded. Otherwise, all other siblings, whether currently living or dead, or whether natural, step, foster, or adoptive have been included. In the case of multiple births as far as possible (in the case register this is specifically asked for), the order of birth is taken as for normal sibships. On the register survey forms, ordinal position and the original numbers of siblings of each sex, irrespective of birth order, are recorded. When no siblings had died, it was possible to obtain the numbers of older brothers and older sisters from the living family members who are listed with their ages. In all other cases it was necessary to send a questionnaire which specifically inquired about older and younger brothers and sisters, whether living or dead. Similar questions were included in the general population questionnaires. As all subjects were aged 20 or older, it is likely that the vast majority of sibships were complete. The assumption has been made that the subjects were, during their childhood, living in the same household as the recorded siblings. Because of the break-up of some families following bereavement, this was clearly not always the case.

RESULTS

The incidence of early bereavement in in-patients and controls

The bereavement data have been considered in detail elsewhere *(Birtchnell* (1971)). In brief, 24.9 % of patients receiving more than one month's inpatient treatment, compared with 20.4 % of the general population controls, had been bereaved of at least one parent before age 20; and 11.1 % of the same in-patient group, compared with 8.6 % of the controls, had been so before age 10. Both these differences are significant: in the first comparison $\chi^2 = 14.2286$, d. f. $= 1$, p $<$ .001, and in the second $\chi^2 = 8.175$, d. f. $= 1$, p<.01. For both age periods the difference remains significant for women considered separately, but not for men; and for mother loss considered separately, but not for father loss.

Comparison of the sibships of early bereaved and not early bereaved inpatients and controls

In Tables 2–9 the early bereaved and not early bereaved in-patients and controls are compared in respect of the size and composition of their sibships. The object of these comparisons is to ascertain whether the familial setting in which the bereavement occurred, rather than the bereavement itself, is a factor which differentiates between the two groups and which may therefore be of aetiological significance.

Table 2 gives the sibship sizes of in-patients and control subjects whose mothers died before the age of 10 and whose mothers were still alive by age 20. The sibship size distribution does not differ significantly between the two-bereaved groups. There is a suggestion that the bereaved women in-patients tend to come from larger sibships than the bereaved men in-patients or the bereaved women controls but the differences are not significant.

Table 3 gives the sibship sizes of the two groups whose fathers died before the age of 10 and whose fathers were still alive by age 20. Again the sibship size distributions of the two bereaved groups are similar and do not differ significantly.

It is perhaps surprising that, for both the in-patients and the control subjects, the sibship size distributions of the early bereaved do not differ significantly from those of the non-bereaved. In both cases, however, as might be expected, the bereaved sibships do tend to be smaller.

Table 4 is concerned with the presence of younger siblings in the mother-bereaved and non-mother-bereaved in-patients and control subjects. The burden of the premature assumption of motherhood in female subjects with younger siblings might be expected to be a factor in mental illness. From the control data it is clear that early mother death results in subjects' having fewer younger siblings: 70.1% of the non-bereaved have younger siblings,

Table 2. *Sibship size distribution of mother-bereaved (age 0–9) and of non-mother-bereaved subjects*

		Sibship size 1	2	3	4	5 or more	Total known about	Not known
Early bereaved								
In-patients (29–84 days)	Men	4 (11.1 %)	5 (13.9 %)	8 (22.2 %)	4 (11.1 %)	15 (41.7 %)	36	3
	Women	4 (7.7 %)	4 (7.7 %)	9 (17.3 %)	6 (11.5 %)	29 (55.8 %)	52	0
	Total	8 (9.1 %)	9 (10.2 %)	17 (19.3 %)	10 (11.4 %)	44 (50.0 %)	88	3
Controls	Men	2 (4.7 %)	9 (20.9 %)	9 (20.9 %)	5 (11.6 %)	18 (41.9 %)	43	1
	Women	3 (5.5 %)	6 (10.9 %)	16 (29.1 %)	5 (9.1 %)	25 (45.5 %)	55	0
	Total	5 (5.1 %)	15 (15.3 %)	25 (25.5 %)	10 (10.2 %)	43 (43.9 %)	98	1
Non-early bereaved								
In-patients (29–84 days)	Men	69 (8.1 %)	103 (12.1 %)	123 (14.5 %)	123 (14.5 %)	431 (50.8 %)	849	31
	Women	54 (4.3 %)	121 (9.7 %)	171 (13.8 %)	186 (15.0 %)	712 (57.2 %)	1244	41
	Total	123 (5.9 %)	224 (10.7 %)	294 (14.1 %)	309 (14.8 %)	1143 (54.6 %)	2093	72
Controls	Men	102 (7.5 %)	192 (14.1 %)	212 (15.5 %)	181 (13.3 %)	678 (49.7 %)	1365	2
	Women	117 (6.6 %)	260 (14.6 %)	270 (15.1 %)	256 (14.4 %)	881 (49.4 %)	1784	10
	Total	219 (7.0 %)	452 (14.4 %)	482 (15.3 %)	437 (13.9 %)	1559 (49.5 %)	3149	12

2 × 5 chi-square (bereaved in-patients: controls) 3.1992, d. f. = 4. N. S.
2 × 5 chi-square (bereaved: non-bereaved in-patients) 4.1132, d. f. = 4. N. S.
2 × 5 chi-square (bereaved: non-bereaved controls) 8.6903, d. f. = 4. N. S.

compared with 64.9 % of those bereaved from age 10 to 19 and only 55.9 % of those bereaved from age 0 to 9. Among the in-patients the early bereaved men show a striking reduction in the number of younger siblings: 52.5 % compared with 70.4 % of the non-bereaved. The early bereaved women, however, show no such reduction and the percentage of early bereaved and non-bereaved with younger siblings is almost identical. Thus 73.0 % of the bereaved women compared with only 52.5 % of the bereaved men have younger siblings. This difference is significant (p < .01). Thus this greater than expected number of bereaved women patients with younger siblings supports the hypothesis that the burden of caring for these younger siblings may

118

Table 3. *Sibship size distribution of father-bereaved (age 0–9) and of non-father-bereaved subjects*

		Sibship size					Total known about	Not known
		1	2	3	4	5 or more		
Early bereaved								
In-patients (29–84 days)	Men	2 (3.7 %)	7 (13.0 %)	7 (13.0 %)	14 (25.9 %)	24 (44.4 %)	54	0
	Women	6 (7.4 %)	9 (11.1 %)	14 (17.3 %)	13 (16.0 %)	39 (48.1 %)	81	2
	Total	8 (5.9 %)	16 (11.9 %)	21 (15.6 %)	27 (20.0 %)	63 ((46.7 %)	135	2
Controls	Men	11 (12.6 %)	8 (9.2 %)	12 (13.8 %)	15 (17.2 %)	41 (47.1 %)	87	0
	Women	8 (8.2 %)	16 (16.3 %)	13 (13.3 %)	11 (11.2 %)	50 (51.0 %)	98	0
	Total	19 (10.3 %)	24 (13.0 %)	25 (13.5 %)	26 (14.1 %)	91 (49.2 %)	185	0
Non-early bereaved								
In-patients (29–84 days)	Men	68 (8.4 %)	98 (12.1 %)	122 (15.0 %)	112 (13.8 %)	411 (50.7 %)	811	33
	Women	50 (4.2 %)	112 (9.4 %)	157 (13.2 %)	175 (14.7 %)	695 (58.5 %)	1189	37
	Total	118 (5.9 %)	210 (10.5 %)	279 (14.0 %)	287 (14.4 %)	1106 (55.3 %)	2000	70
Controls	Men	92 (7.2 %)	188 (14.6 %)	205 (15.9 %)	167 (13.0 %)	634 (49.3 %)	1286	3
	Women	108 (6.5 %)	240 (14.4 %)	255 (15.3 %)	242 (14.6 %)	818 (49.2 %)	1663	10
	Total	200 (6.8 %)	428 (14.5 %)	460 (15.6 %)	409 (13.9 %)	1452 (49.2 %)	2949	13

2×5 chi-square (bereaved in-patients: controls) 3.8198, d. f. = 4. N. S.
2×5 chi square (bereaved: non-bereaved in-patients) 4.9169, d. f. = 4, N. S.
2×5 chi-square (bereaved: non-bereaved controls) 3.8111, d. f. = 4, N. S.

have contributed to their illness. Among the bereaved control subjects the percentages for men and women are more alike. Patients and controls differ most during the earlier 0–9 age span where the figure of 72.5 % for the women patients contrasts markedly with that for the men and for the ccntrols.

Table 5 is concerned with the presence of younger siblings in the father-bereaved and non-father-bereaved in-patients and control subjects. This time one would predict that the premature assumption of the paternal role in male early father-bereaved patients should result in a greater proportion of male patients having younger siblings. As with early mother death, it will be seen that the early death of a father also results in a diminution in the

Table 4. *The percentage of mother-bereaved and non-mother-bereaved with younger siblings (the percentages are of known cases)*

Age at death of mother	In-patients (29–84 days)				
	Men	N/K	Women	N/K	Total
0–9	18/36	3	37/51	1	55/87
	(50.0 %)		(72.5 %)		(63.2 %)
10–19	24/44	2	52/71	1	76/115
	(54.5 %)		(73.2 %)		(66.1 %)
Total early mother-bereaved	42/80	5	89/122	2	131/202
	(52.5 %)		(73.0 %)		(64.9 %)
Not early mother-bereaved	588/835	45	906/1232	53	1494/2067
	(70.4 %)		(73.5 %)		(72.3 %)

Patients: controls/with younger siblings: without younger siblings
(0–19) $\chi^2 = 0.4547$, d. f. = 1, N.S.
Similar comparison (0–9) $\chi^2 = 0.7149$, d. f. = 1, N.S.
Patients, men:women/with younger siblings: without younger siblings (0–19)
$\chi^2 = 7.0412$, d. f. = 1, p <.01.
Controls, men:women/with younger siblings: without younger siblings
(0–19) $\chi^2 = 0.8746$, d. f. = 1, N.S.

Table 5. *The percentage of father-bereaved and non-father-bereaved with younger siblings (the percentages are of known cases)*

Age at death of father	In-patients (29–84 days)				
	Men	N/K	Women	N/K	Total
0–9	38/52	1	52/81	2	90/133
	(73.1 %)		(64.2 %)		(67.7 %)
10–19	32/60	3	59/96	4	91/156
	(53.3 %)		(61.5 %)		(58.3 %)
Total early father-bereaved	70/112	4	111/177	6	181/289
	(62.5 %)		(62.7 %)		(62.6 %)
Not early father-bereaved	555/798	46	885/1176	50	1440/1974
	(69.5 %)		(75.3 %)		(72.9 %)

Patients: controls/with younger siblings: without younger siblings
(0–19) $\chi^2 = 1.0580$, d. f. = 1, N.S.
Similar comparison (0–9) $\chi^2 = 7.4731$, d. f. = 1, p <.01.
Men patients: women patients/with younger siblings: without younger siblings (non-bereaved) $\chi^2 = 7.5578$, d. f. = 1, p <.01.

ntrols

en	N/K	Women	N/K	Total
2/40	4	30/53	2	52/93
5.0 %)		(56.6 %)		(55.9 %)
7/62	1	50/72	1	87/134
9.7 %)		(69.4 %)		(64.9 %)
9/102	5	80/125	3	139/227
7.8 %)		(64.0 %)		(61.2 %)
6/1332	34	1241/1745	48	2157/3077
8.8 %)		(71.1 %)		(70.1 %)

ontrols

en	N/K	Women	N/K	Total
40/86	1	54/96	2	94/182
6.5 %)		(56.3 %)		(51.6 %)
1/94	2	96/153	0	157/247
4.9 %)		(62.7 %)		63.6 %)
1/180	3	150/249	2	251/429
6.1 %)		(60.2 %)		(58.5 %)
1/1252	36	1175/1621	51	2046/2873
9.6 %)		(72.5 %)		(71.2 %)

Table 6. *The percentage of mother-bereaved and non-mother-bereaved with no older sister (the percentages are of known cases)*

Age at death of mother	In-patients (29–84 days)				
	Men	N/K	Women	N/K	Total
0–9	17/36 (47.2 %)	3	23/48 (47.9 %)	4	40/84 (47.6 %)
10–19	14/41 (34.1 %)	5	22/64 (34.4 %)	8	36/105 (34.3 %)
Total early mother-bereaved	31/77 (40.3 %)	8	45/112 (40.2 %)	12	76/189 (40.2 %)
Not early mother-bereaved	398/770 (51.7 %)	110	502/1142 (44.0 %)	143	900/1912 (47.1 %)

Patients: controls/without older sister: with older sister (0–19)
$\chi^2 = 3.3339$, d. f. = 1, N.S.
Similar comparison (0–9) $\chi^2 = 2.3770$, d. f. = 1, N.S.
Men patients: women patients/ without older sister: with older sister (non-bereaved) $\chi^2 = 10.7230$, d. f. = 1, p < .005.

Table 7. *The percentage of father-bereaved and non-father-bereaved with no older brother (the percentages are of known cases)*

Age at death of father	In-patients (29–84 days)				
	Men	N/K	Women	N/K	Total
0–9	21/47 (44.7 %)	6	33/77 (42.8 %)	6	54/124 (43.5 %)
10–19	20/54 (37.0 %)	9	39/91 (42.9 %)	9	59/145 (40.6 %)
Total early father-bereaved	41/101 (40.6 %)	15	72/168 (42.9 %)	15	113/269 (42.0 %)
Not early father-bereaved	370/739 (50.1 %)	105	491/1084 (45.3 %)	142	861/1823 (47.2 %)

Patients: controls/with no older brother: with older brother (0–19)
$\chi^2 = 2.0581$, d. f. = 1, N.S.
Similar comparison (0–9) $\chi^2 = 0.2315$, d. f. = 1, N.S.
Table 6 plus Table 7: either-bereaved, patients: controls/without older sibling of the same sex as the lost parent: with such a sibling (0–19)
$\chi^2 = 5.0050$, d. f. = 1, p < .025.
Similar comparison (0–9) $\chi^2 = 1.9818$, d. f. = 1, N.S.

en	N/K	Women	N/K	Total
3/40	4	20/54	1	33/94
2.5 %)		(37.0 %)		(35.1 %)
4/62	1	24/72	1	38/134
2.6 %)		(33.3 %)		(28.4 %)
7/102	5	44/126	2	71/228
6.5 %)		(34.9 %)		(31.1 %)
8/1334	32	853/1752	41	1471/3086
6.3 %)		(48.7 %)		(47.7 %)

en	N/K	Women	N/K	Total
30/87	0	43/95	3	73/182
34.5 %)		(45.3 %)		(40.1 %)
31/95	1	52/153	0	83/248
32.6 %)		(34.0 %)		(33.5 %)
51/182	1	95/248	3	156/430
33.5 %)		(38.3 %)		(36.3 %)
38/1261	27	745/1621	51	1333/2882
46.6 %)		(46.0 %)		(46.3 %)

123

Table 8. *The percentage of mother-bereaved and non-mother-bereaved with no older sister and with younger siblings (the percentages are of known cases, i. e. information must be known about both older sister and younger siblings)*

Age at death of mother	In-patients (29–84 days)				
	Men	N/K	Women	N/K	Total
0–9	10/36 (27.8 %)	3	19/48 (39.6 %)	4	29/84 (34.5 %)
10–19	10/41 (24.4 %)	5	16/64 (25.0 %)	8	26/105 (24.8 %)
Total early mother-bereaved	20/77 (26.0 %)	8	35/112 (31.3 %)	12	55/189 (29.1 %)
Not early mother-bereaved	292/768 (38.0 %)	112	395/1142 (34.6 %)	143	687/1910 (36.0 %)

Patients: controls/with no older sister and with younger siblings: remainder (0–19) $\chi^2 = 3.4874$, d. f. = 1, N. S.
Similar comparison (0–9) $\chi^2 = 2.5447$, d. f. = 1, N.S.
Women patients: women controls/with no older sister and with younger siblings: remainder (0–19) $\chi^2 = 1.5551$, d. f. = 1, N.S.
Similar comparison (0–9) $\chi^2 = 2.6488$, d. f. = 1, N.S.

Table 9. *The percentage of father-bereaved and non-father-bereaved with no older brother and with younger siblings (the percentages are of known cases, i. e. information must be known about both older brother and younger siblings)*

Age at death of father	In-patients (29–84 days)				
	Men	N/K	Women	N/K	Total
0–9	16/47 (34.0 %)	6	23/77 (29.9 %)	6	39/124 (31.5 %)
10–19	10/54 (18.5 %)	9	30/91 (33.0 %)	9	40/145 (27.6 %)
Total early father-bereaved	26/101 (25.7 %)	15	53/168 (31.5 %)	15	79/269 (29.4 %)
Not early father-bereaved	269/739 (36.4 %)	105	392/1084 (36.2 %)	142	661/1823 (36.3 %)

Patients: controls/with no older brother and with younger siblings: remainder (0–19) $\chi^2 = 2.3534$, d. f. = 1, N.S.
Similar comparison (0–9) $\chi^2 = 2.1607$, d. f. = 1, N.S.
Men patients: men controls/with no older brother and with younger siblings: remainder (0–19) $\chi^2 = 0.5477$, d. f. = 1, N.S.
Similar comparison (0–9) $\chi^2 = 3.1643$, d. f. = 1, N.S.

ontrols

Men	N/K	Women	N/K	Total
9/40 (22.5%)	4	12/53 (22.6%)	2	21/93 (22.5%)
9/62 (14.5%)	1	17/72 (23.6%)	1	26/134 (19.4%)
18/102 (17.6%)	5	29/125 (23.2%)	3	47/227 (20.7%)
55/1330 (34.2%)	36	630/1744 (36.1%)	49	1085/3074 (35.3%)

Controls

Men	N/K	Women	N/K	Total
16/86 (18.6%)	1	26/95 (27.4%)	3	42/181 (23.2%)
22/94 (23.4%)	2	38/153 (24.8%)	0	60/247 (24.3%)
38/180 (21.1%)	3	64/248 (25.8%)	3	102/428 (23.8%)
17/1251 (33.3%)	37	581/1617 (35.9%)	55	998/2868 (34.8%)

Table 8 plus Table 9: either-bereaved, patients: controls/with no older sibling of the same sex as lost parent and younger siblings: remainder (0–19) $\chi^2 = 5.6850$, d. f. = 1, p < .02.

Similar comparison (0–9) $\chi^2 = 5.1413$, d. f. = 1, p < .025.

Either-bereaved subjects of the same sex as the lost parent, patients: controls/with no older sibling of the same sex as lost parent and younger siblings: remainder (0–19) $\chi^2 = 2.6524$, d. f. = 1, N.S.

Similar comparison (0–9) $\chi^2 = 7.1714$, d. f. = 1, p < .01.

proportion of control subjects who have younger siblings: 71.2 % of the non-bereaved have younger siblings compared with 63.6 % of those bereaved from age 10 to 19 and only 51.6 % of those bereaved from age 0 to 9. The in-patients show a different pattern. Though those bereaved from age 10 to 19 have substantially fewer younger siblings than those not early bereaved, 58.3 % compared with 72.9 %, those bereaved from age 0 to 9 have almost as many, 67.7 %. Because of this, within the 0 to 9 age span, there are significantly more bereaved patients than controls with younger siblings (p < .01).

The proportion of male patients bereaved during this period who have younger siblings is higher even that of the not early bereaved ones. Once more the trend is in the expected direction and supports the proposed hypothesis. An unexpected finding is that, among the non-bereaved in-patients, significantly more women than men have younger siblings (p < .01).

Table 6 is concerned with the absence of an older sister in the mother-bereaved and non-mother-bereaved in-patients and control subjects. It might be argued that mother bereavement would be more disturbing to those with no older sister for (1) they would have no sister to serve as partial replacement for the lost mother and (2) they themselves might be expected, by both the remaining father and the younger siblings, to accept the role of replacement mother. From the control data it appears that early bereaved subjects tend to have more older sisters than those who are not. Those bereaved from age 10 to 19 have most. The same situation is apparent among the in-patients though to a lesser degree. This is related to the fact that more bereaved patients than controls have no older sister, which is as would be anticipated. That the difference is no greater for female patients suggests that lack of a parent substitute, rather than the need to act as substitute parent to younger siblings, is the more important aspect of this situation. Again there is an unexpected difference between the non-bereaved men and women patients: significantly more women have older sisters (p < .005).

Table 7 is concerned with the absence of an older brother in father-bereaved and non-father-bereaved in-patients and control subjects. As with early mother death the early bereaved appear to have more older brothers, and those bereaved from age 10 to 19 have most. The situation is once more less apparent among the in-patients and this again is related to there being more bereaved patients than controls with no older brother. The difference is no greater for male patients.

The findings of Tables 6 and 7 are in the same expected direction: the patients have fewer older siblings of the same sex as the lost parent and in this respect differ significantly from the controls (p < .025).

Tables 8 and 9 combine the features of Tables 4 to 7. It might be expected that being the oldest sibling of the same sex as the lost parent and having younger siblings to look after would impose the greatest strain; and therefore in this respect the patients should differ from the controls to the most marked extent. In Table 8 early mother-bereaved and non-mother-bereaved subjects with no older sister but with younger siblings are considered. From the control data it will be seen that a smaller proportion of the early mother-bereaved have no older sisters but also younger siblings. Once again, the lowest incidence is among those bereaved from age 10 to 19. The same situation obtains for the in-patients. However, the difference is less marked for the patients, so that more patients have this particular sibship combination. The most striking difference between patients and controls occurs in the 0 to 9 age span and, as would be expected, it is most pronounced for the women patients.

In Table 9 early father-bereaved and non-father-bereaved subjects with no older brother but with younger siblings are considered. As before, a smaller proportion of the early father-bereaved have this sibship combination, but the proportions in the 0 to 9 and 10 to 19 age spans who have it are similar. The patients again show a higher incidence. The difference between patients and controls is most marked among those bereaved from age 0 to 9 and again, as would be expected, is particularly so for the men.

Thus the findings of Tables 8 and 9 follow the same pattern: there are significantly more early bereaved patients with no older sibling of the same sex as the lost parent and with younger siblings ($p < .02$). The difference between patients and controls is most marked when the parent of the same sex as the patient has died during the 0 to 9 span ($p < .01$).

DISCUSSION

It is more than ten years since *Hilgard, Newman & Fisk* (1960), in a mainly descriptive study, attempted to elucidate the factors which might modify the effects of early bereavement. They compared the life situations of 240 early bereaved individuals from the local community with those of an early bereaved patient group. Though their reports have the ring of authenticity, it is disappointing that neither they nor subsequent workers have provided statistical confirmation of the hypotheses put forward. They stated, for instance, that "in one form of social pathology, the surviving parent becomes so emotionally dependent upon the children that the child finds it difficult to make a normal separation from the parent when he himself becomes an adult." They considered that men whose fathers had died were involved in this type of interdependency to a marked degree far more than women. They observed, "The mothers felt that they were needed by their grown children, and in some cases this was indeed true, because the mother's continued concern had perpetuated childhood patterns." However, not only is it likely that the remaining parent will turn towards the children for solace and gratification, but that the children will turn towards each other, such that younger siblings will readily see older ones as parent figures and the older ones will respond to this appeal in a parental manner. The thesis of the present study is that siblings who have no such older sibling to turn to will be worse off than those who have and those who have younger siblings which turn to them will be subjected to greater stress than those who have not.

To obtain a sufficiently large number of early bereaved individuals it has been necessary to start with large samples of subjects. Although data on 6,795 psychiatric patients were available, it was decided to include in this study only the smaller number of 2,407 who had spent at least a month in hospital. It was felt that, though this would reduce the number of early bereaved patients to approximately 500, this restriction to a more seriously ill group would be more likely to reveal factors which might differentiate between patients and controls.

A consequence of selecting the in-patient subsample in this way is that the patient group has been made significantly older than the control group. *Price & Hare* (1969) pointed out that, due to the variation over the years in rates of reproduction, the chances of being early or late born vary with decade of birth. The difference in the sibships of the early bereaved patients and early bereaved controls may therefore merely reflect such differences in the patients and controls anyway, because of differences in birth year distribution. To be certain that this was not the case, it was necessary to examine the sibships of the subjects in the two groups whose parents did not die before they were aged 20, though they might have died later.

The differences which were observed between the early bereaved patients and the controls were predominantly in the direction anticipated from the stated hypotheses. Even though the numbers of cases in the categories selected were small, in a number of instances the differences were statistically significant. Similar differences were not manifest in the non-bereaved patient and control groups and the incidences of the various sibship characteristics in these two groups were strikingly similar. In the instances where there were differences they were not in the same direction as those between early bereaved patients and controls. It would appear therefore that the characteristics of the sibships of the early bereaved patients do differ from those of the early bereaved controls. Since no such differences in the sibships of the non-bereaved patients and controls are apparent, it is clear that these differences are peculiar to the early bereaved.

Having ascertained this point, it is reasonable to consider the implications of the findings. It is probably true, particularly in large families, that the older siblings assume some parental responsibility towards the younger ones. Older sisters become deputy mothers and older brothers deputy fathers. As a

128

result of this such older siblings may well identify with the same sexed parent to a more marked degree than the younger ones. In turn, the opposite sexed parent may come to see them in this way. Thus on the death of a parent such latent relationships will naturally emerge and become strengthened. In this familial rearrangement it is a matter for speculation as to which of the family members are most disturbed. Consideration of the remaining parent has not been included in the present study. *Parkes* (1964, 1965) has described the reaction of spouses to bereavement and *Hilgard, Newman &* *Fisk* (1960), *Fast & Cain* (1963), and *Gates, Roff & Stiver* (1965) have suggested that the relationship between the remaining spouse and the children may be seriously affected. There is, however, need for more carefully planned investigations in this important area. Of the siblings, it is unclear whether it is the older ones who carry the premature burden of the care of the younger ones or the younger ones who suffer from the imperfect handling of the ill-prepared older ones who are most at risk, as suggested by *Rosenbaum* (1963). The present findings suggest that the presence of a replacement "parent sibling" is better than none and that being that "parent sibling" with younger siblings to care for is worse than not being such a sibling.

The control data have demonstrated the effects of early bereavement on the constitution of normal sibships. The percentage of subjects with younger siblings and with no older siblings of the same sex as the lost parent (and this presumably applies to older siblings in general) is considerably reduced, among both the early mother-bereaved and the early father-bereaved. These findings presumably arise from the fact that parents are more likely to die towards the end of their reproductive years. It seems probable that the early bereaved subjects tend to come from the later birth ranks of their sibships and that the sibships tend to be smaller than normal. This difference in the sibship size and composition of the early bereaved and non-early bereaved subjects is less marked in the patient sample because proportionally larger numbers have younger siblings and proportionally fewer have older ones of the same sex as the lost parent. As a result of this there is a closer correspondence between the sibships of the early bereaved and non-early bereaved patients.

In most of the comparisons the age period 0 to 9 appears to be the more crucial one, when differences between the patient and the control group are most marked. This may be because this is the period during which the incidence of early bereavement differs most between the two groups. Thus as loss of a parent has a significant effect only during this period it is also only during the same period that the sibship setting in which the loss occurred is important. It might be argued that a child under age ten can hardly be capable of acting as parent to younger siblings. It must be remembered, however, that, from the moment of parent loss, the sibship composition remains unchanged, with the exception, of course, of the acquisition of step-siblings: so that the oldest sibling of the appropriate sex will, over the years, take on progressively more parental responsibility at a time when he or she is ill able to cope with it and is deprived of parental care too.

The children shown to be most at risk in the present study are those with no older siblings of the same sex as the lost parent and those with younger siblings. Such children will tend to be the earliest born ones. An alternative explanation for the findings may be that such children have particularly close relationships with their parents as parents may lavish more affection upon their earliest born children. As a consequence of this, such children may suffer a greater sense of loss when either parent dies. The fact that more mother-bereaved female than male patients and more father-bereaved male than female patients have younger siblings suggest that this is not the most satisfactory explanation.

Two incidental findings among the non-early bereaved subjects, that significantly more men patients have older sisters and significantly more women than men have younger siblings, have not been discussed in this study. They are a birth order effect and will be considered in a separate publication. It is sufficient for the purpose of the study that they do not contribute to the differences observed between early bereaved in-patients and controls.

SUMMARY

The study is part of a large investigation of familial factors in mental illness, utilizing samples of 6,795 psychiatric referrals to the North-Eastern region of Scotland and 3,425 subjects from the general population. A subsample of 2,407 patients, who received more than 28 days in-patient treatment, has been extracted to represent a severely ill group.

Significantly more of the in-patient subsample, compared with the control group, had been bereaved of at least one parent before age 20 ($p < .001$) and before age 10 ($p < .01$). The size and composition of the sibships of the early bereaved and non-early bereaved in-patients and controls has been compared in order to ascertain whether the family setting, within which the bereavement occurred, was a factor determining whether the subjects might subsequently develop a mental illness.

The control data suggest that early parental bereavement is associated with diminution in the proportion of subjects with younger siblings but an increase in the proportion with older ones. This presumably is due to the fact that parents are more likely to die towards the end of their reproductive period.

The size of the sibship appears to be somewhat reduced by early bereavement. The sibship size distribution of the early bereaved in-patients and controls did not differ significantly.

There were, as anticipated, more early mother-bereaved women patients and early father-bereaved men patients with younger siblings in comparison to the control group.

There were, again as anticipated, fewer mother-bereaved patients with older sisters and fewer father-bereaved patients with older brothers in comparison to the control group.

There were more early mother-bereaved women patients with no older sister and with younger siblings and more early father-bereaved men patients with no older brother and with younger siblings.

The findings of the study tend to confirm, therefore, that the presence of an older sibling of the same sex as the lost parent alleviates the adverse effect of early bereavement but that being such a sibling enhances them.

ACKNOWLEDGEMENTS

A preliminary report on this study was presented in a paper to the Psychiatry Section of the Royal Society of Medicine in April, 1970. The study was carried out during the tenure of a Medical Research Council Clinical Research Fellowship. It forms part of a larger investigation of a variety of familial factors in mental illness involving the North-Eastern Regional Psychiatric Case Register and a local population control group. I am indebted to Dr. *John Baldwin* for his assistance in planning and carrying this out and to Mr. *John Evans* for organizing the Aberdeen computer search. I would like to thank Mrs. *Linda Wilson* for checking the stored data and for her help in arranging its transfer from Aberdeen to the MRC Computer Unit in London. Dr. *C. C. Spicer*, Director of the Unit, devised a programme for the analysis of the data and the analyses were carried out by Mrs. *Angela Mott*. I am most grateful to Prof. *Ian Richardson*, Director of the General Practice Teaching and Research Unit, Aberdeen, and the general practitioners of the North-Eastern Region for their generous co-operation in the general population survey. I should also like to thank the technical and clerical staff of the Mental Health Research Unit (Aberdeen) and a number of temporary research assistants, who were paid by a supplementary grant from the MRC, for their help in the tedious collection and preparation of the data. Finally I should like to express my appreciation of the encouragement and advice of Dr. *Peter Sainsbury* and other members of the MRC Clinical Psychiatry Unit in Chichester.

REFERENCES

Arthur, B., & *M. Kemme* (1964): Bereavement in Childhood. J. Child Psychol. 5, 37–49.

Baldwin, J. A., G. Innes, W. M. Millar, G. A. Sharp & *N. Dorricott* (1965): A Psychiatric Case Register in North-Eastern Scotland. Brit. J. prev. soc. Med. 19, 38–42.

Birtchnell, J. (1969): Parent Death in Relation to Age and Parental Age at Birth in Psychiatric Patients and General Population Controls. Brit. J. prev. soc. Med. 23, 244–250.

Birtchnell, J. (1971): A Case-Register Study of Bereavement. Proc. roy. Soc. Med. 64, 279–282.

Brown, F. (1966): Childhood Bereavement and Subsequent Psychiatric Disorder. Brit. J. Psychiat. 112, 1035–1041.

Cain, A., & *B. Cain* (1964): On Replacing a Child. J. Amer. Acad. Child. Psychiat. 3, 443–456.

Dennehy, C. (1966): Childhood Bereavement and Psychiatric Illness. Brit. J. Psychiat. *112,* 1049–1069.

Fast, I., & *A. Cain* (1963): Disturbances in Parent-Child Relationships Following Bereavement. Paper read to the American Psychological Association.

Fast, I., & *A. Cain* (1966): The Step-parent Role: Potential for Disturbances in Family Functioning. Amer. J. Orthopsychiat. *36,* 485–491.

Freud, A. (1960): Discussion of Dr. John Bowlby's Paper. Psychoanal. Stud. Child. *15,* 53–62.

Gates, P., C. Roff & *I. Stiver* (1965): Studies of the Significance of Death of a Parent for Young Children: A Preliminary Report. Paper read to 42nd Annual Meeting of the American Orthopsychiatric Association.

Gregory, I. (1958): Studies of Parental Deprivation in Psychiatric Patients. Amer. J. Psychiat. *115,* 432–442.

Gregory, I. (1966): Retrospective Data Concerning Childhood Loss of a Parent. Arch. gen. Psychiat. *15,* 362–367.

Hilgard, J., M. Newman & *F. Fisk* (1960): Strength of Adult Ego Following Childhood Bereavement. Amer. J. Orthopsychiat. *30,* 788–798.

Kaufman, I., A. Peck & *C. K. Tagiuri* (1954): The Family Constellation and Overt Incestuous Relations between Father and Daughters. Amer. J. Orthopsychiat. *24,* 266–279.

Messer, A. A. (1969): The Phaedra Complex. Arch. gen. Psychiat. *21,* 213–218.

Munro, A. (1969): The Theoretical Importance of Parental Deprivation in the Aetiology of Psychiatric Illness. Appl. Soc. Stud. *1,* 81–92.

Parkes, C. M. (1964): Recent Bereavement as a Cause of Mental Illness. Brit. J. Psychiat. *110,* 198–204.

Parkes, C. M. (1965): Bereavement and Mental Illness. Brit. J. med. Psychol. *28,* 13–26.

Price, J., & *E. Hare* (1969): Birth Order Studies. Some Sources of Bias. Brit. J. Psychiat. *115,* 633–646.

Rosenbaum, M. (1963): Psychological Effects on the Child Raised by an Older Sibling. Amer. J. Orthopsychiat. *33,* 515–520.

Parental Bereavement in Childhood : M.M.P.I. Profiles in a Depressed Population

By IAN C. WILSON, LACOE B. ALLTOP and W. J. BUFFALOE

Recent studies of childhood bereavement in depressive populations (Forrest, Fraser, and Priest, 1965; Munro, 1966) indicate that parental bereavement in childhood may be of aetiological significance in depressive illness (Forrest et al., 1965) and may affect the severity of the clinical picture (Munro, 1966).

During the past year we have been collecting behavioural and biological data in a depressed population with the specific aim of predicting the therapeutic outcome with imipramine therapy. These data included an M.M.P.I. profile (Hathaway and McKinley, 1951) and a detailed history of childhood bereavement.

Recently published studies of childhood bereavement in psychiatric populations (Forrest et al., 1965; Munro, 1966; Hopkinson and Reed, 1966; Greer, 1966) prompted us to analyse our M.M.P.I. data according to the presence or absence of childhood bereavement.

METHOD

Patient Population: The depressed patients studied were 100 consecutive admissions, men and women aged 60 years or less, admitted to Unit 5, Dorothea Dix Hospital, Raleigh, North Carolina. Selective criteria were similar to those used in previous drug studies (Wilson et al., 1963; Wilson et al., 1964; Sandifer et al., 1965) with the specific aim of selecting only "primary" depressions (Kline, 1961). Care was taken to

exclude specifically the following: depression
secondary to schizophrenia, drug addiction,
alcohol addiction, sociopathic personality or
organic disease of the central nervous system.
Local studies have shown a high level of
diagnostic agreement in placing individual
patients in the diagnostic group of primary
depressions (Sandifer, Pettus, and Quade,
1964).

M.M.P.I. Administration: The full M.M.P.I.,
in card form, was administered to the individual
patient during the first twenty-four hours of
admission to hospital. Eight patients were
unable to complete this test generally as a result
of severe retardation or severe agitation. Of
these eight patients one had a history of parental
bereavement in childhood and seven had not.

Childhood bereavement: For the purpose of
this study, childhood bereavement is defined as
the death of either parent before the patient was
aged 16 years. This information was obtained
from the patient at the first clinical interview.

Before analysis of the data, the following
hypotheses were formulated: (a) The childhood
bereaved group of patients would have higher
mean scores in the basic scales of the M.M.P.I.
than the non-bereaved group; (b) In the
childhood bereaved group, those patients who
had maternal loss would have higher basic scale
scores than those patients who had paternal
loss.

RESULTS

Of the 92 patients who were able to complete
the M.M.P.I., 28 patients gave a history of
bereavement of either or both parents before the
age of 16 years.

Table I shows the distribution of type
parental death by sex of the patient.

TABLE I

Incidence of Parental Bereavement According to Sex of Patient

	Maternal Loss	Paternal Loss	Loss of Both Parents
Female patients	7	7	3
Male patients	3	7	1
Totals	10	14	4

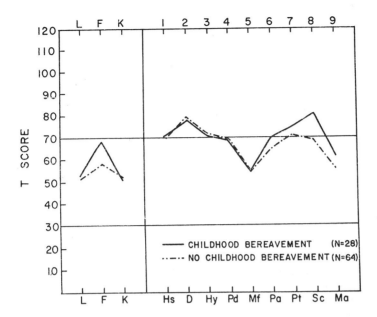

FIG. I.—Mean Standard Scores on M.M.P.I. Childhood Bereavement vs. No Childhood Bereavement.

Table II shows the mean standard scores of the M.M.P.I. scales according to the presence or absence of childhood bereavement. Fig. I shows the same data illustrated graphically.

In the childhood bereaved group there is a more marked elevation of the F score on the validity scales. In the basic scales both groups show remarkably similar scores in the neurotic triad (Hs, D, and Hy) (McKinley and Hathaway, 1944), but in the psychotic tetrad (Pa, Pt, Sc, Ma) (Gough, 1946; Dahlstrom and Welsh, 1960) differences occur between the two populations. The childhood bereaved group having higher scores in all these scales especially the Sc scale. Both populations show diphasic curves in the basic scales with an overall "neurotic" type negative slope in the non-

135

TABLE II

Mean Standard Scores of M.M.P.I. Scales
Childhood Bereaved vs. Non-Childhood Bereaved

	Validity Scales			Basic Scales								
	L	F	K	Hs	D	Hy	Pd	Mf	Pa	Pt	Sc	Ma
Non-bereaved (N=64)	52·0	58·1	52·1	68·9	78·6	71·0	69·6	54·0	64·1	70·8	68·4	55·9
Bereaved (N=28)	52·7	68·2	50·6	70·4	77·2	70·7	68·8	54·9	69·4	74·2	80·1	69·0

TABLE III

Mean Standard Scores on M.M.P.I. Scales
Childhood Bereaved Group: Loss of Father vs. Loss of Mother

	Validity Scales			Basic Scales								
	L	F	K	Hs	D	Hy	Pd	Mf	Pa	Pt	Sc	Ma
Loss of Father (N=14)	54·5	69·6	52·0	68·0	74·6	68·2	68·0	54·9	68·1	68·1	78·7	60·8
Loss of Mother (N=10)	51·6	70·9	47·8	74·5	80·7	72·0	71·1	53·8	72·5	82·1	86·4	65·9

bereaved population and an overall "psychotic" type positive slope in the bereaved group (Hovey, 1949).

The t-test was the method employed to determine significant differences between the two populations on individual scales.

The means of the F scale $(t=3 \cdot 57)$ and the Sc scale $(t=3 \cdot 10)$ were significantly different at the five per cent. level of probability. The trends of the bereaved group being higher on the Pa, Pt, and Ma scales are suggestive of true differences but did not quite reach the level of significance at the five per cent. level of probability.

Table III shows the mean standard scores on the M.M.P.I. scales for the childhood bereaved population divided into two groups according to whether there was paternal or maternal bereavement in childhood.

In all of the basic scales except Mf the maternally bereaved group have higher mean scores than the paternally bereaved group. In total scores this finding is significant at the five per cent. level of probability. Both populations show positively sloped biphasic curves (Hovey, 1949).

DISCUSSION

Our data suggest that there are differences in M.M.P.I. profiles between two depressed populations divided according to the presence or absence of parental bereavement in childhood: the non-bereaved group having a "neurotic" profile; the bereaved group having a "psychotic" profile. The significantly higher F score in the bereaved group would lead one to emphasize the more elevated scales on the psychotic end of the profile of this group (Kazan and Sheenberg, 1945). This study gives further substance to Munro's concept that childhood bereavement will increase the severity of a depression if it occurs (Munro, 1966).

Our second hypothesis was confirmed, namely, that there would be a more severe disturbance in M.M.P.I. profile in the maternally bereaved population than in the paternally bereaved group. It is interesting to note that differences occur in both the neurotic triad and the psychotic triad in these two populations.

As the M.M.P.I.s were administered within the first twenty-four hours of admission to hospital, it is possible that the differences between the two groups represent a transient situational reaction to the stress of admission to hospital and loss of family relationships. It has been reported that the (F) score is sensitive to stress situations (Brozek and Schiele, 1948). It could be postulated that the bereaved group responded to the stress more acutely because the loss of family reactivated the previous pattern of behaviour defined by parental bereavement.

Summary

The M.M.P.I. profiles of 92 consecutive depressed admission patients were analysed according to the presence or absence of parental bereavement in childhood. The parentally bereaved group showed higher scores in the psychotic tetrad. In the childhood bereaved group the mean scores on the basic scales of those who had lost their mother were uniformly (except for the Mf scale) and significantly higher than the mean scores for those who had lost their father.

References

Brozek, J., and Schiele, B. C. (1948). "Clinical significance of the Minnesota Multiphasic F. Scale evaluated in experimental neurosis." *Amer. J. Psychiat.*, **105**, 259–266.

Dahlstrom, W. G., and Welsh, G. S. (1960). *An M.M.P.I. Handbook*. Minneapolis: University of Minneapolis Press.

Forrest, A. D., Fraser, R. H., and Priest, R. G. (1965). "Environmental factors in depressive illness." *Brit. J. Psychiat.*, **111**, 243–253.

Gough, H. G. (1946). "Diagnostic patterns on the M.M.P.I." *J. clin. Psychol.*, **2**, 23–37.

Greer, S. (1966). "Parental loss and attempted suicide: A further report." *Brit. J. Psychiat.*, **112**, 265–470.

Hathaway, S. R., and McKinley, J. C. (1951). *Minnesota Multiphasic Personality Inventory*. Psychol. Corp., New York.

Hopkinson, G., and Reed, G. F. (1966). "Bereavement in childhood and depressive psychosis." *Brit. J. Psychiat.*, **112**, 459–463.

Hovey, H. B. (1949). "Somatization and other neurotic reactions and M.M.P.I. profiles." *J. clin. Psychol.*, **5**, 153–156.

Kazan, A. T., and Sheenberg, I. M. (1945). "Clinical note on the significance of the valdity score (F) in the M.M.P.I." *Amer. J. Psychiat.*, **102**, 181–183.

KLINE, N. S. (1961). "Depression: diagnosis and treatment." *Med. Ann. N. Amer.*, 45, 1041–1053.

McKINLEY, J. C., and HATHAWAY, S. R. (1944). "The M.M.P.I: Hysteria, hypomania and psychopathic deviate." *J. applied Psychol.*, 28, 153–174.

MUNRO, A. (1966). "Parental bereavement in depressive patients." *Brit. J. Psychiat.*, 112, 443–457.

SANDIFER, M. G., PETTUS, C. W., and QUADE, D. (1964). "A study of psychiatric diagnosis." *J. nerv. ment. Dis.*, 139, 350–356.

—— WILSON, I. C., and GAMBILL, J. M. (1965). "The influence of case selection and dosage in an antidepressant drug trial." *Brit. J. Psychiat.*, 111, 142–148.

WILSON, I. C., GAMBILL, J. M., and SANDIFER, M. G. (1964). "A double blind study comparing imipramine (Tofranil) with desmethylimipramine (Pertofran)." *Psychosomatics*, 5, 88–91.

—— VERNON, J. T., GUIN, T., and SANDIFER, M. G. (1963). "A controlled study of treatments of depression." *J. Neuropsychiat.*, 4, 331–337.

PARENTAL DEPRIVATION IN CHILDHOOD
AND TYPE OF FUTURE MENTAL DISEASE

Ole Bratfos

It is a current contention that parental deprivation and "broken home" predispose to mental disease in adult age. The issue has been treated by many authors. A common procedure has been to investigate how often psychiatric patients have grown up deprived of mother, father, or both—and to compare the incidence with that in a control group. The control data originate from many sources: From population statistics, or a material of mentally healthy individuals, from non-psychiatric patients, or from psychiatric patients with other diagnosis than the actual subjects. The conclusions have been controversial but, according to *Bowlby* (1952), a clear tendency emerges from the literature: Loss of one or both parents in childhood is more frequent for mental patients than in the ordinary population.

However, in many of the investigations the result seems somewhat uncertain due to methodological problems (*Gregory* 1958, and others). An important question is whether the patient group and the control material are commensurable with reference to factors which may influence the frequency of parental deprivation or "broken home"—such as domicile, social status, religion, age of the patient, and the parents' age. Another point is that the pertinent information on the patients comes from medical quarters, whereas the controls have usually answered the corresponding questions in quite another situation. Possible discrepancies in the findings may then be accounted for by a different motivation for answering the questions adequately.

When comparing patients with different mental disorders, or using these as mutual controls, the methodological problems do not enter the picture to the same degree. Then the question is not whether psychiatric patients have lost their parents more often than mentally healthy persons, but whether the incidence of parental deprivation is higher in one form of mental disturbance than in another.

Studies comparing the findings in two or more mental disorders are scarce. *Barry* (1949) investigated 1683 psychotic and 330 neurotic patients. In both groups about 7 per cent of the patients had lost father or mother by death before 8 years of age. *Denneby* (1966) studied 1020 patients—schizophrenics, depressive patients, alcohol and drug addicts—and found that the incidence of childhood bereavement was approximately the same for the different diagnoses. *Oltman et al.* (1952) describes childhood conditions for 1451 individuals, mainly schizophrenics but also cases of neurosis, psychopathy, alcoholism, manic-depressive psychosis, and a group of mentally healthy persons. The authors include all forms of separation, temporary as well as permanent. Close to 50 per cent of the patients with neuroses and psychopathy had lost mother and/or father before 19 years of age, whereas the incidence for patients with psychoses was the same as for the mentally healthy group, viz. slightly over 30 per cent. *Greer* (1964) compared 79 cases of "sociopathy", 387 cases of neurosis, and 691 normal controls with reference to parental deprivation lasting for more than 12 months before 15 years of age. The rates were 60 per cent, 28 per cent, and 27 per cent respectively.

As far as a difference has been demonstrable, parental deprivation seems to be more frequent in psychopathies than in the other diagnostic groups. Also investigations comprising only one diagnostic category (and control group) suggest that persons with social adjustment difficulties have often grown up without mother and/or father. Scandinavian works show a relatively high incidence of parental deprivation for criminals (*Mögelstue* 1962), for maladjusted adolescents and children (*Frey* 1944, *Otterström* 1946, *Ekblad* 1948, *Christie* 1960, *Jonsson* 1967) and for alcoholics (*Åmark* 1951, *Brun-Guldbrandsen* & *Irgens-Jensen* 1964). In neuroses (*Ljungberg* 1957, *Kringlen* 1965) and psychoses (*Stenstedt* 1952, *Nielsen* 1954, *Retterstöl* 1966) the incidence is on the whole lower—according to some of the authors, probably not very different from that in the ordinary population.

Whether the parental deprivation is due to death, divorce, or illegitimate birth may be of importance. The literature is not abundant on this point and in most cases limited to study of children and adolescents with different kinds of adjustment failure. In the majority of these studies, there is no definite relation between loss of parents by death and the maladjustment. On the other hand, deprivation of mother and/or father due to the parents not being married, or to divorce is a fairly common finding. Thus *Ekblad* (1948) in a study of 995 naval conscripts found that those who had adjustment problems in the service were often born out of wedlock or came from divorce homes. Death of parents seemed of little consequence in this connection. The same tendency appears from *Christie's* (1960) investigation on 562 juvenile delinquents. Up to about 14 years of age, 10.5 per cent of the youths had lost mother and/or father, whereas 5.0 per cent of the parents were separated or divorced—against 9.3 per cent and 1.8 per cent respectively in the control material. *Jonson's* (1967) material comprises 305 boys confined to reformatories. Of these, 7 per cent had lost one or both parents by death, while as many as 57 per cent lacked one or both parents due to illegitimacy or divorce.

The corresponding figures for the "normal group" were 5 per cent and 18 per cent respectively.

THE PRESENT INVESTIGATIONS

The present study was designed to investigate and compare the frequency of "broken home" for patients with different psychiatric diagnoses. The concept of "broken home" covers cases in which the deprivation of one or both parents has been permanent due to the parents not being married, to divorce, or to death of one or both parents before the patient was 15 years old. Separation from parents for other reasons, for instance protracted hospital stays, are thus not included.

The case records of 4000 patients admitted to the Psychiatric Department, University of Oslo, during the years 1959–1965 have been reviewed. The age ranges from 14 to 81 years with mean and median of 40.4 and 39.9 years respectively. Age distribution appears from Table 1. As the hospital accommodates the same number of male as of female patients, sex distribution is is even (49.9 per cent male, 50.1 per cent female).

With reference to civil status, 34.0 per cent of the patients were single, 59.0 per cent married, 3.7 per cent separated or divorced, while 3.3 per cent were widowed. The Psychiatric Department takes in patients from all over the country. In the present material the bulk of the patients—74.5 per cent— are from rural districts, 19.4 per cent from small towns, and only 6.1 per cent live in a city (i. e. Oslo). The patients' occupational status has been used to indicate their socio-financial background (Table 2). Housewives are listed under their husbands' occupation.

A total of 721, or 18.0 per cent, of the 4000 patients had lost one or both parents in childhood. In 6.4 per cent of the cases the father was dead, in 4.9

TABLE 1

Patients grouped according to age, indicated in per cent

Age in years	No. of patients = 4000
	%
19 and less	6.3
20–29	20.6
30–39	23.5
40–49	24.4
50–59	16.2
60–69	8.1
70 and more	0.9
	100.0

TABLE 2

*Patients grouped according to occupation,
indicated in per cent*

Occupation	No. of patients = 4000
	%
Industrial and transport workers .	30.4
Forestry, agricultural, fish workers, housemaids	11.2
Artisans	5.8
Farmers	9.5
Independent tradesmen	5.0
Small employees	26.1
Higher employees, } University men }	3.6
Pupils, students	5.9
Other	2.5
	100.0

per cent the mother was dead, and in 0.2 per cent both parents had died (total 11.5 per cent). For 3.5 per cent of the patients, the separation from mother and/or father was due to illegitimacy, whereas divorce was the cause for 3.0 per cent.

Table 3 shows the discharge diagnoses together with the number of patients within the separate diagnostic groups lacking mother, father, or both. The diagnostic criteria indicated by *Langfeldt* (1965) have been used. The diagnoses of manic-depressive psychosis and schizophrenia are based on *Kraepelin*'s definition. As reactive psychoses are counted disorders in which an interplay between personality and conflicts may have precipitated a psychotic reaction. "Other psychoses" represent a composite group, mainly comprising cases where the differential diagnosis have wavered between different "functional" psychoses. Minor mental disorders in which the causal connection appeared to be mainly psychogenic have been classed as neuroses. The further subgrouping has been determined according to predominant symptom (like anxiety or depression) or according to assumed pathogenesis or "dynamics" (hysteriform or character neurosis). The group psychopathy mainly comprises patients whose marked personality deviation has led to social adjustment difficulties. Alcoholism, narcomania, and organic brain disorder should need no further definition. The last group in Table 3 is partly made up of different types of disease with only a few patients within each form and, partly, by patients so briefly admitted that exact diagnosis was not possible.

The frequency of parental deprivation for the separate diagnostic groups deviates little from the mean, i. e. 18 per cent. Only the group psychopathy stands out clearly, 31.4 per cent of these patients having had to do without mother and/or father for a shorter or longer part of their childhood. This tallies

143

with the findings of other investigators. As could be expected, the incidence is fairly high for the category narcomania/alcoholism too, but the group is small. All the neurotic subgroups are close to the mean, taken together, 388 of 2100 patients—or 18.5 per cent—have lost one or both parents in childhood. The incidence of parental deprivation is relatively low in all forms of psychosis, 185 of 1211 patients, or 15.3 per cent, having lost one or both parents. For the patients with organic brain disorder, the incidence is 16.5 per cent. To seek a connection between childhood conditions and an organic disorder, often developing at a late stage of life, seems rather far-fetched and these patients might therefore be regarded as a "normal material". With good support in the the literature, the findings in Table 3 might then be interpreted as follows: The incidence of parental deprivation is not higher for psychoses than in the ordinary population and only moderately increased for the neuroses, whereas there is a definite increase for the groups alcoholism/narcomania and for psychopathies. Calculation according to the χ^2 test indicates that there is a real difference ($p < 0.05$) between the psychoses and the neuroses and also between the neuroses and the psychopathies ($p < 0.001$), but that the difference is not significant between the neuroses and alcoholism/narcomania ($p > 0.05$).

We shall now consider the factors which may influence the frequency of parental deprivation, e. i. sex, age marital status, domicile, and social status. Are these fairly evenly distributed over the various diagnostic groups? As far as can be seen from the case records, the psychotic and the neurotic groups

TABLE 3

Frequency of parental loss in childhood, indicated in per cent for the different diagnostic groups

Diagnoses	Total No. of patients	Loss of mother/father No.	Loss of mother/father % of total No.
Schizophrenia	131	20	15.3
Reactive psychosis	540	84	15.6
Manic-depressive psychosis	235	32	13.6
Other psychoses	305	49	16.1
Neurosis, anxiety	421	80	19.0
Neurosis, hysteriform	553	91	16.5
Neurosis, depressive	720	141	19.6
Neurosis, compulsive	74	13	17.6
Neurosis, neurastheniform	175	31	17.7
Neurosis, character	157	32	20.4
Psychopathy	188	59	31.4
Alcoholism/narcomania	80	21	26.3
Organic brain disorder	206	34	16.5
Sundry	215	34	15.8
	4000	721	(mean 18.0)

TABLE 4

Loss of father and/or mother by death compared with deprivation due to non-marriage or divorce, indicated in per cent

Diagnosis	No.	Dead %	Non-married divorced %	Total %
Psychosis	1211	10.9	4.4	15.3
Neurosis	2100	11.3	7.2	18.5
Psychopathy	188	15.4	16.0	31.4
Others	501	11.6	6.2	17.8
	Mean:	11.5	6.5	18.0

do not differ greatly from the total material on any of these counts. The group alcoholism/narcomania, on the other hand, is too small to allow of reliable comparison, and in the group psychopatics the number of young patients is relatively high—36.0 per cent are under 25 years of age against 15.5 per cent in the total material. This makes evaluation of the relative position of the psychopathies somewhat problematical.

The next question is whether parental deprivation due to death and parental deprivation due to illegitimacy or divorce seem to have affected the findings in Table 3 to different degree. To avoid too low figures the material has been divided into two categories only, i. e. "parents dead" and "parents non-married or divorced" and the diagnostic groups have been confined to "psychosis", "neurosis", "psychopathy", and "others". The findings appear from Table 4.

A total of 457 out of 4000 patients, or 11.5 per cent, had lost one or both parents by death. As seen from Table 4, the percentages for the separate diagnostic groups deviate but slightly from the mean for the total material, although the rate is highest for the psychopathy group. The difference is not statistically significant, however ($p > 0.05$). One may thus say that loss of parents by death is about equally frequent for the psychotic, neurotic, and psychopathic groups.

In 264 cases, or 6.5 per cent, the parents had not been married or they were divorced. Here the deviation from the mean percentage is more marked. The frequency of non-married and divorced parents is lowest for psychosis, higher for neurosis, and highest for psychopathy. The tenability of this finding is borne out by calculations according to the χ^2 method. The difference between the psychoses and the neuroses is significant at the 0.1 per cent level and between the neuroses and the psychopathies at the 1 per cent level. The uneven distribution of patients with non-married or divorced parents fully seems to account for the differences appearing in Table 3.

The findings in Tables 3 and 4 suggest that, even though the frequency of parental deprivation varies but little between the separate diagnostic groups, certain differences emerge: The incidence is lowest for the psychoses, slightly higher for the neuroses, and definitely highest for the psychopathies. These differences do not reflect death of parents, but are due to illegitimacy and divorce.

DISCUSSION

Undue weight should not be placed on the absolute figures for how often the patients' parents have been non-married, divorced, or have died. The information from the case records will probably not always quite meet the case. However, the main purpose of the present study has been to examine the *relation* between the diagnoses.

It is a precondition for comparing the rates for the different diagnostic groups that there has been no systematic error in the collection of the information. One might ask whether the anamnestic data for the neuroses and the psychopathies could be more complete than for the psychoses so that a difference in the occurrence of the actual childhood conditions would have to be expected. But the difference in the sampling would then have affected the findings if the parents were non-married or had been divorced only, and not if they had died. That seems hardly likely.

One might further ask whether the relatively high figures for parental deprivation for neuroses and psychopaties might be due to a special selection with reference to hospitalization. In psychotic conditions, the manifestations of the disease are frequently of a type to necessitate hospitalization. In more moderate mental disturbances, admission to hospital may not always be as necessary. Then an uncertain family situation may decide whether or not the patient should be admitted to hospital—maybe especially in the case of a single parent with a teen-ager with adjustment difficulties. The above mentioned study by *Jonsson* (1967) may serve as an illustration of this. He found that more than half of the boys confined to reformatories were illegitimate or their parents were divorced. One might then ask what has been most decisive for the confinement—the delinquency or the family background?

Another possibility is that some patients with reaction patterns warranting the diagnosis of neurosis and, more particularly, of psychopathy come from environments where illegitimate birth and divorce are a fairly common occurrence. On the other hand, special selection mechanism(s) need not be decisive and an overrepresentation of "broken home" in some types of mental disease might have a direct causal connection with the respective diseases. To have a child out of wedlock or to divorce, may be regarded as being maladjusted to the norms of the environment. Looking at it in this way, the parents' particular type of weakness might conceivably result in adjustment failure in the next generation too, and in that generation be interpreted as "neurosis" or "psychopathy". Such a connection may be claimed to be hereditary. A psychogenetic explanation assuming that parental deprivation causes a deviating personality development is, however, more usual. Then the individual might be unfit for working through later occurring traumae and conflicts—and manifest disease might develop as a consequence. However, with reference to psychogenesis the question is not only whether "broken home" *predisposes* to mental disturbances—even more often it may represent a *precipitating* factor. Loss of one or both parents may, immediately or after some time, involve an unbearable life situation and give rise to nervous reactions in the child or adolescent. This is borne out by the fact that in studies on children and adolescents a preponderance of parental deprivation is a common finding, whereas the results for adult patients may seem rather less convincing.

Above has been discussed some possible interpretations of the results of the present investigation. There are arguments in favour of various possibilities and it is difficult to arrive at definite conclusions. The findings indicate that parental deprivation is more frequent for neuroses and for psychopathies than for psychoses. Are we confronted with special selection mechanism(s) without causal connection between childhood conditions and type of later mental disease? Is there a causal connection and, if so, what is the mechanism? It is not possible to answer these questions on the basis of the present investigation.

SUMMARY

The case records for 4000 patients admitted to the Psychiatric Department, University of Oslo, have been reviewed with regard to occurrence of parental deprivation in childhood through death, non-marriage, or divorce. Of the 1211 patients with psychoses, 15.3 per cent had lost mother and/or father. For the 2100 patients with neuroses, the rate was 18.5 per cent. The incidence was highest for the psychopathic group in that 31.4 per cent of the 188 patients had lost one or both parents.

The difference between the separate diagnostic groups as to frequency of "broken home" is largely due to illegitimacy or divorce, whereas loss of parents by death is fairly evenly distributed over the diagnostic groups.

REFERENCES

Barry, H. (1949): Significance of maternal bereavement before age of eight in psychiatric patients. Arch. Neurol. Psychiat. (Chic.) *62*, 630–637.

Bowlby, J. (1952): Maternal care and mental health. World Health Organization, Geneva.

Brun-Gulbrandsen, S., & *O. Irgens-Jensen* (1964): Alkoholmisbruk blant unge norske sjömenn. Universitetsforlaget, Oslo.

Christie, N. (1960): Unge norske lovovertredere. Universitetsforlaget, Oslo.

Denneby, C. M. (1966): Childhood bereavement and psychiatric illness. Brit. J. psychiat. *112*, 1049–1069.

Ekblad, M. (1948): A psychiatric and sociologic study of a series of Swedish naval conscripts. Acta psychiat. scand. Suppl. *49.*

Frey, T. S. (1944): Om vanart hos flickor i Stockholm. Svenska Läk.-Tidn. *41,* 1701–1711.

Greer, S. (1964): Study of parental loss in neurotics and sociopaths. Arch. gen. Psychiat. *11,* 177–180.

Gregory, I. (1958): Studies of parental deprivation in psychiatric patients. Amer. J. Psychiat. *115,* 432–442.

Jonsson, G. (1967): Delinquent boys, their parents and grandparents. Acta psychiat. scand. Suppl. *195.*

Kringlen, E. (1965): Obsessional neurotics. A long-term follow-up. Brit. J. Psychiat. *111,* 709–722.

Langfeldt, G. (1965): Lærebok i klinisk psykiatri. Aschehoug, Oslo.

Ljungberg, L. (1957): Hysteria. A clinical, prognostic and genetic study. Acta psychiat. scand. Suppl. *112.*

Möglestue, I. (1962): Kriminalitet og sosial bakgrunn. Statistisk Sentralbyrå, Oslo.

Nielsen, C. K. (1954): The childhood of schizophrenics. Acta psychiat. scand. *29,* 281–289.

Oltman, J. E., J. J. McGarry & *S. Friedman* (1952): Parental deprivation and the "broken home" in dementia praecox and other mental disorders. Amer. J. Psychiat. *108,* 685–694.

Otterström, E. (1946): Delinquency and children from bad homes. Lindstedt, Lund.

Retterstöl, N. (1966): Paranoid and paranoiac psychoses. Universitetsforlaget, Oslo.

Stenstedt, Å. (1952): A study in manic-depressive psychosis. Acta psychiat. scand. Suppl. *79.*

Åmark, C. (1951): A study in alcoholism. Acta psychiat. scand. Suppl. *70.*

PARENTAL LOSS AND SOME CHARACTERISTICS OF THE EARLY MARRIAGE RELATIONSHIP

Gary Jacobson, M.D. and Robert G. Ryder, Ph.D.

The literature on the later effects of losing a parent is abundant. A history of parental loss has been associated with psychoneurosis,[6] suicide,[11] alcoholism and narcotic drug addiction,[5] schizophrenia,[7] depressive illness,[9] anxiety reactions,[2] sociopathic character and criminal behavior,[4] poor employment record,[8] and failure in the Peace Corps.[12] Many of these studies deal with loss from separation, divorce, or death without distinguishing among them. Looking specifically at the effects of bereavement at a young age, Barry and Lindemann [1] summarized their clinical material as follows: "If married, they were so afraid of losing their family/that their spouses and their children felt safe in making unreasonable demands of the patient, who then reacted with outward submissiveness and inward resentment and depression." Others [10] have described "the inability to let anyone else care," "shallow and meaningless relationships," and "the fear of letting anyone else get to know them." A minority view holds that while parental divorce and separation are significant, parental death has not been demonstrated to be a factor in psychopathology regardless of parent lost or the age that loss occurred.[3]

By and large, one is left with the impression that a history of parental death will probably be associated with severe trouble in the early years of marriage, a time when issues of trust, separation, autonomy, and sexuality are encountered with great intensity. We were therefore surprised when studying a group of 30 couples selected because they were exceptionally close, had relative freedom with intimacy and communication, and enjoyed each other to an unusually full extent, to find that the incidence of parental death prior to marriage in these couples was 40%, twice that of the entire volunteer pool from which they had been drawn. It was this curious finding which led us to the present search for the variety of marriage outcomes associated with a death in the family of origin and some of the factors involved.

METHOD

A test sample of 90 couples with a history of parental death prior to marriage and a control sample of 30 couples with no history of parental loss from any source were drawn from a population of 1,200 couples who were paid volunteers in a study of early marriage. These subjects were American born, in their first marriage, married for two and a half years or less, between 18 and 25 for the wife and 20 to 27 for the husband, living in the Washington, D. C. area, and included both white and Negro couples.

The subjects were seen for a total of approximately seven hours on three separate occasions. A battery of information-gathering and personality tests were administered, and joint and individual interviews were held. Ratings were made by the interviewer and an observer. For more intensive studies, certain couples were chosen for group interviews and role-playing inprovisations. Among the parameters to which particular attention was paid were interpersonal closeness, the handling of anger, and sexuality.

In our population of couples with loss, four marriage types or syndromes seem to stand out:

1. The first syndrome to be described is the "closeness, late loss syndrome." The median age of loss for this group was 17, with all but three experiencing the loss during adolescence. Of our loss sample, 13.3% exhibited this syndrome, characterized by the following:

The marriage relationship was clearly central to these couples. There was a great degree of closeness, depth, or intimacy, feelings of openness of communication, feelings of gratitude for the spouse, and a feeling of family reconstitution. They see their having found each other as a stroke of good fortune.

They tend to see themselves as a largely self-contained unit and judge their actions according to the satisfactions they derive rather than according to a notion of normalcy or convention. They are not invested in conspicuously flouting convention; rather they seem not especially concerned with it.

Couples in this group used words such as these to describe their relationship: unique, sensitive, fun, mutual, honest, complete, responsible, unconventional, ultimate.

There was no overall suppression of anger. However, there was a marked commitment, often explicit, to limit the duration of anger or argument. None of the couples reported arguments lasting overnight; most said that their arguments lasted less than half an hour and often only a few minutes. Arguments were frequently terminated by one spouse responding to a display of sadness from the other and noting that the issue "was not worth it." The issue was, however, generally brought up again a few hours or days later, either to explore it seriously or to dispose of it in a playful way.

Affect regarding loss of a parent was in general easily available in the interview and the relationship with the parent was recalled as a particularly good one.

Mrs. M was talking volubly about the happiness of her relationship with her husband when suddenly she came almost to tears when questioned about the death of her father at age 13. She recalled how much she had missed her father and she thought that she had learned because of this loss not to take too seriously any defects or difficulties but to bear in mind what really counted was "not having the relationship die completely."

The interviewers felt the spouses as individuals to be likeable and self-examining. The husbands, compared to other husbands, seemed remarkably at ease with tenderness. Sexual experiences for these couples were satisfying and without major problems.

2. The second syndrome is characterized by the loss of wife's parent in mid-adolescence and the wife having a

marked inability to enjoy sexual relations in an otherwise close marriage. 18.5% of couples with a loss of wife's parent after age 12 (N=27) fit this pattern, with about half having lost a father and half a mother. The median age at loss was 16.

In these marriages, the husband tends to be caretaking at home and steady at work. Although he is disturbed by his wife's unresponsiveness, he is seen as being forbearing and patient by her. Both wish the situation to improve but feel helpless to have it do so.

Mr. and Mrs. B expressed a feeling of gratitude for having found one another, felt they had grown enormously during the five months of their marriage, and were extremely pleased with their independence and their high acceptability by friends and employers. After a week or two of mildly enjoyable sexual relations, wife ceased having any sensations whatsoever and looked at sexual relations as a task to be given in to, distasteful and to be feared, although she had no reasons why. Her mother had died when she was 16, approximately four years prior to her marriage. In conversation she revealed the fantasy that now she was in the position of being a mother, identified with her own mother and felt fearful. for her own life. In addition she talked about the seductive manner of her father before and especially after her mother's death, and her extreme guilt in responding to this in fantasy, although not in actuality. She felt that since her mother was not present it was particularly disloyal to have felt the way she did, and these feelings were again aroused during the sexual play prior to intercourse. She returned for three followup interviews and in the last interview, which was held together with her husband, she said that the situation had modified itself dramatically and that for the first time since her honeymoon she was beginning to enjoy sexual relations.

3. The third syndrome is comprised of couples in which the husband's father has died and the husband's struggle with dependency and identity are prominent in the marriage relationship. 15% of couples with a history of loss of hus-

153

band's father (N=40) made up this syndrome, and the median age of loss was 8.

The following is a composite profile of the husband in these marriages: He is a pseudo-optimist: "I never worry about anything. This worries my wife, that bothers me." He uses jokes and teasing to avoid confrontation but is able to break out of this and support his wife solidly if she is in trouble. He is heavily involved with female pursuits, such as housekeeping and cooking and is hypercritical of his wife in these regards. There is less sexual activity than desired by wife. He is capable of sustaining warmth and is appreciative when he receives it. He acknowledges his wish to be "spoiled" but is ambivalent about being "too thoughtful." Anger is more easily triggered, and he both sulks more profoundly and erupts more noisily than the couples described above. Arguments may result in silence for a day or two and there is more likely to be physical violence such as hitting or throwing things, or the threat of it such as reckless driving. Following the argument, solidarity is increased more by the knowledge that the relationship has withstood the crisis than by understanding the issues. The same issue in the same form is likely to repeat itself although diminish in frequency. In the interview, affect does not change when talking about his father, although he may talk about his mother with enthusiasm. He is sometimes flamboyant in his presentation, sometimes mildly depressed, but almost always cagey. He feels things are better than ever before in his life and he doesn't want to rock the boat.

4. In the fourth syndrome, characterized by early loss and chronic conflict,

there is difficulty in developing and almost total failure in sustaining intimacy. 11% of our loss sample comprise this syndrome. The median age at loss was 7, about half the losses being mothers and half fathers.

These marriages are seen as being shaky and uncertain. Sexual relations are intermittantly enjoyed and often avoided. Husband insists on one or more nights out a week to "protect his independence" and spends them with old unmarried friends, usually male.

Anger is prolonged for several days or weeks and marked by separations of several hours or more. Anger is terminated by fatigue, diversion, or capitulation but almost never by agreement. Other people are often brought into the argument, particularly parents of relatives, but sometimes friends as well. After termination of arguments, the marriage partners feel relieved but suspicious. The spouse with the loss usually feels deprived, restless, and trapped. The spouse without the loss usually feels guilty, bewildered, and then trapped as well.

These marriages are obviously in profound difficulty. The following words were used by one of these couples to describe their relationship: Husband: love, hate, war, peace, satisfaction. Wife: rocky, wild, understanding, contempt, loyalty. Rage and ambivalence are clearly illustrated. In this particular couple there was a struggle towards a better relationship, but in others the marriage was conceded to be on the verge of ending.

CLINICAL ISSUES

The following examples are not presented as marriage syndromes but as a

155

sampling of issues encountered in couples with a history of loss.

Interference with the development of the marriage relationship, and the confusion of affect which comes from having both to mourn one close relationship and to celebrate another at the same time, was strikingly apparent in the following marriage which took place when loss was acute.

Two weeks before her wedding, Mrs. A's father was hospitalized and died. Four months into the marriage she finds herself increasingly preoccupied with thoughts of separation, abandonment, and her own annihilation. She now cries frequently and has begun to be overly concerned with any activity that might involve risk, such as driving a car or even walking across the street. She would like to reach out to her husband but feels unable to do so. Most important, she misses not having any really romantic feelings about him which she vaguely remembers having had some time in the past. In her marriage she often feels she is an innocent victim of a fast-talking and unfamiliar man.

In couples with loss, fears of dying or losing the spouse were frequently explicit and in several instances took the form of asking the spouse at the time of marriage to promise that he or she would never die or leave. These feelings typically began around the time of agreement to marry, or a few months after marriage together with a growing feeling of dependency. These fears, although sometimes recurrent, were generally circumscribed. The following unusual couple has made fear of death and separation, defenses against these eventualities, and attempts to master old losses, a central focus of their marriage.

Mr. O's father died when O was 14, after a year's illness. Husband's only remark about the loss is that it allowed him the satisfaction of being able to finance his own education. Shortly after the death he became, and still remains, a student of one of father's music

156

students. Wife's parents, both living, had prepared to divorce about the time of her engagement but did not follow through.

Mr. and Mrs. O's house is filled with pets—dogs, mice, fish—which husband purchases and helps care for with the fantasy that his wife is peculiarly sensitive and vulnerable to the loss of these pets, in fact potentially more upset by the loss of a pet than if he himself should die.

Both of his automobiles have names, first, middle, and last names. His avocation is to keep them in repair. He talks about them as follows: "They were pretty old when I bought them but I brought them back from the graveyard." He goes on to blend animate and inanimate losses: "I tell my wife to be careful every day but what if she has been in an accident and needs help, aid, or comfort? If she or her car should be hurt or killed, I would worry because the car would be totally destroyed and I couldn't rebuild it. If you look after a machine a certain length of time, the machine has a way of looking after you."

His wife supports this blurring of distinction between life and nonlife and for Christmas gave him a nine-volume study of idols.

The attitude of one marriage partner toward the loss of a parent by the other partner varies widely. Most commonly, the fact of loss is considered peripheral. "I already have parents, I married to get a wife. It would be nice for her to have two parents but it really doesn't matter to me." Often there is a protective attitude: "She really has no one to turn to but me so we better be certain we work out our differences and not let them get out of hand." If the spouse is free enough regarding his own feelings toward loss, there are opportunities in early marriage to help the other toward coming to terms with residual fears, longing, and sadness. This seems especially true in the process of resolving anger and threats of separation. In the close couples we have seen, much of this work occurs before marriage and is one of the factors in deepening the relationship.

Around the time of marriage there is often a reawakening of interest and fantasy regarding a parent lost many years previously. This was often expressed simply as: "I wish he (or she) were here to see how well I am doing." The following is an example of the slow revival of interest in a parent after 10 years of suppression.

Mr. F's father died when F was 11 years old. Although he can remember certain events around the funeral, he has almost total amnesia about his father. He recalls going out to play football the day following father's death and in retrospect feels this was not the proper way for him to act. He did not go to the funeral, although he does not know why. From time to time he has looked at his father's picture and recognizes him only because he has been told this is a picture of father. Most of what he remembers about his father he has been told. He has a feeling that his 15-year-old sister was supposed to have been distraught by father's death, but "no one ever told me it was traumatic for me." He says this with some resentment as if he has been cheated out of this aspect of closeness with father.

At around the time of engagement it occurred to him that his wife's birthday in November was the same day on which his father died. Before that he had not thought about his father for a long time. During the four months of his marriage he has become disturbed about his lack of knowledge of his father and has become aware that in the past he had been putting off thinking about his father and had been denying feelings. There were some clues in the interview that suppression of memory was so strong because of the fantasy that he may have contributed to father's death. In pondering about whether he was actually close or distant with father, he noted that he was appointed the "executioner" of his father's will upon turning 21. This slip was immediately changed to "executor."

His marriage is a very satisfactory one. He feels that it is his position of relative security and ease in talking with his wife that has permitted him the freedom to go back and open up some rather frightening areas.

158

While difficulty in separation from the family of origin is by no means limited to spouses with a loss, the common reality that the remaining parent is being left alone makes the issue more complicated.

Mrs. R's father died 1½ years prior to her marriage. As long as her mother seemed despondent, ill, or angry, Mrs. R called her daily, with a feeling of resentful obligation. In the rare instances when her mother hinted at being cheerful or seemed to be enjoying herself with her new suitor, Mrs. R attempted to break away by not calling at all. Three or four days later, her mother would call again despairing and expressing her preference for daughter's company to that of anyone else. Her husband felt put off by her mother's demandingness, was frightened by her pessimism, and was not much help to his wife. This situation has produced two sets of plans for Mrs. R. One is to try to help mother more intensively and the other is to move to another state.

Guilt about abandonment of the surviving parent often intensifies Oedipal issues as well.

Mr. L's father died when L was 17, and he lived at home until his marriage at age 21. In a common variety of the Oedipal situation, Mr. L felt obliged to have weekly outings with his mother and wife. His mother felt displaced and angry, his wife felt undefended and unhappy, and he, while adamantly continuing to set up the situation, felt victimized.

Mr. U attempted to solve this situation before marriage. He persuaded an old male friend of the family to move in with his mother. When this seemed to work all too well, he turned to wooing not only his wife but also his mother-in-law. Despite, or perhaps because of, valentine presents, flowers, etc., mother-in-law remained reserved in her affections. After one year, among the major themes of the marriage is the husband's fury about not being fully accepted by mother-in-law.

MARRIAGE CLOSENESS AND AGE AT LOSS

Evidence for marriage closeness consisted of good verbal communication even in areas of difficulty, enjoyment and pleasure in being together and doing together, absence of problems where little hope is held for solution, feelings of knowing or understanding the other and feelings of intimacy or depth in the relationship, and the marriage relationship usually taking precedence over other considerations such as jobs, friends, or extended family.

Evidence of distance consisted of poor verbal communication, relative absence of pleasure or avoidance of being together, feelings of puzzlement or concern about the other feelings, aloofness, presence of major problems with little hope about solving them, anger often unresolved or of long-term duration, and outside activities given preference frequently enough so that the other spouse considered himself ignored, rejected, or bewildered. If there was not specific evidence for a given item, it went into a nonratable category. The highest possible ratings for closeness on the scale constructed from these items was 5 and the lowest —5.

The mean score for the entire loss group was 1.04 (s=2.22) and for the control group 0.27 (s=1.77), p<.06. The difference is just under the conventionally accepted level for statistical significance. In general, regardless of the sex of spouse or of the parent lost, the scores for marriage closeness were significantly higher for those who lost a parent after age 12 than for those whose loss was between birth and age 12 (TABLE 1). The one exception is that for wives with a loss of father, no difference was found between those whose loss was before 12 and those whose loss was after 12.

Table I

RATINGS OF MARRIAGE CLOSENESS
IN COUPLES WITH PARENTAL LOSS PRIOR TO MARRIAGE
(scale range +5 to −5)

PARENT LOST	AGE OF SPOUSE AT LOSS 0–12		AGE OF SPOUSE AT LOSS Over 12		P [a]
	Mean	s	Mean	s	
Husband's father	0.0	(2.58)	1.95	(2.46)	.002
Husband's mother	−0.71	(1.89)	0.89	(3.18)	.05
Wife's father	1.27	(2.15)	1.46	(1.71)	NS
Wife's mother	0.50	(3.10)	2.00	(2.14)	.015

[a] By the Mann-Whitney U Test.

INCIDENCE OF CHILDREN

Among our loss couples 6.6% did not want any children, compared to none in our control couples. Many of those wanting no children said they liked children but that to have them would be a responsibility and a burden and could not compensate for what would have to be given up in life. Others were afraid that they or the children might get hurt or injured.

More striking, however, was the extent to which couples with loss did want children. Many men, regardless of whether they had lost a father of a mother, considered the potential of their wives as future mothers as a primary factor in selecting them as mates. Not only were the loss couples anxious to have children but they actually did have children far more frequently than control couples. 59% of the loss couples compared to 33% of the control couples had children by 27 months of marriage ($p < .05$). An additional inspection of a small group of couples which lost a parent under the age of 16, showed a similar tendency. 81% of those couples had children by 27 months compared to 37% in the controls ($p = .01$). These differences were not accounted for by racial, religious, or socioeconomic factors.

DISCUSSION AND SUMMARY

About one out of five couples in our study population drawn from the community had experienced the death of a parent prior to marriage. It has been our intention to demonstrate the range of what may be encountered in couples with such a history during the first two and a half years of marriage by describing some of the most frequent clinical outcomes and a number of illustrative phenomena.

Some of these outcomes are marriages with many difficulties, largely substantiating the consensus of the literature. That we were also able to describe quite successful marriage outcomes may be due to the fact that our sample was drawn from the community and not from a patient population as in many of the previous studies.

In the marriage types or syndromes described, there is a general relationship between the ability to sustain intimacy and the age at loss although not with the sex of the parent lost. Manifestations of anger, particularly duration and mode of resolution, are similarly related to age at loss. Impairment of sexual enjoyment in women with close marriages may be just as severe or even more severe than in women with chronically conflicted marriages. However, as seen in close marriages, sexual problems seem to be related to a fairly well-circumscribed resurgence of Oedipal conflicts previously accentuated by the death of a parent and are not related to the vicissitudes of the marriage relationship.

Couples with loss seem to show two extremes regarding children. A small number expressed a wish to have no children whatsoever. The loss population as a whole, however, had significantly more children than the control group.

In the usual development of the marriage relationship, the process of loss and the process of replacement goes on simultaneously. Loss is incomplete and can be regulated. Indeed, in a general realignment of identity and emotional investment, many people choose to come closer to their families of origin soon after marriage. No such gradual processes are available to those who lose a parent by death. Loss is catastrophic, complete, and fully outside the control of the child. In our sample nonetheless, a significant number of these children, particularly adolescents, go on to form stable and particularly close marriage relationships.

In speculating about how this may occur, let us examine the position of the adolescent who loses a parent. His or her fears that the remaining parent will die and he or she will be left totally abandoned and helpless are buffered by already developed independent skills and a network of peer relations and institutions. Guilt and anger at being left may be mitigated if the relationship prior to loss was reasonable and if the loss did not take place after chronic family discontent as it does in divorce. There is a sexual confrontation with the surviving parent but by this time sexual allegiances have already been established beyond the family. In short, the adolescent has social and developmental means, not available to children of younger ages, of handling some of the repercussions that follow the loss of a parent. Acute grief subsides but what about the feeling of longing and loneliness for the parent as a person, the wish for the relationship? We would suggest that there is no adequate resolution of these feelings for the adolescent and several years later he draws from this pool of feelings his hunger for interpersonal closeness in marriage and perhaps also his desire to reconstitute a family as quickly as possible by having children.

REFERENCES

1. BARRY, H., AND LINDERMANN, E. 1965. Dependency in adult patients following early

maternal bereavement. J. Nerv. Ment. Dis. 140:196–206.

2. BOWLEY, J. 1962. *In* Aspects of Psychiatric Research, B. Richter, J. Tanner, L. Taylor, and O. Pangwell, eds.: 262. Oxford Univ. Press, London.

3. BRILL, N., AND LISTON, E. 1966. Parental loss in adults with emotional disorders. Arch. Gen. Psychiat. 14:307–314.

4. BROWN, F. 1966. Childhood bereavement and subsequent psychiatric disorders. Brit. J. Psychiat. 112:1035–1141.

5. DENNEHY, C. 1966. Childhood bereavement and psychiatric illness. Brit. J. Psychiat. 112:1049–1069.

6. GAY, M., AND TONGE, W. 1967. The late effects of loss of parents in childhood. Brit. J. Psychiat. 113:753–759.

7. GRANVILLE-GROSSMAN, K. 1966. Early bereavement and schizophrenia. Brit. J. Psychiat. 112:1027–1034.

8. HALL, P., AND TONGE, W. 1963. Longstanding continuous unemployment in male patients with psychiatric symptoms. Brit. J. Prev. and Soc. Med. 17:191–196.

9. HILL, O., AND PRICE, J. 1967. Childhood bereavement and adult depression. Brit. J. Psychiat. 113:743–751.

10. KRINSKY, A. 1968. Some thoughts on loss in childhood. *In* The Loss of Loved Ones: The Effect of Death in the Family on Personality Development, D. Moriarity, ed.: 148. Charles C Thomas, Springfield, Ill.

11. ROBINS, E., SCHIMIDT, E., AND O'NEAL, P. 1957. Some interrelationships of social factors and clinical diagnoses in attempted suicide. Amer. J. Psychiat. 114:221–231.

12. SUEDFELD, P. 1967. Paternal absence and overseas success of Peace Corps volunteers. J. Consulting Psychol. 4:424–425.

Children's Reactions to Bereavement

Adult Confusions and Misperceptions

Saul I. Harrison, MD; Charles W. Davenport, MD; and John F. McDermott, Jr.

T HIS REPORT was conceived during the course of a study of the response to President Kennedy's assassination involving children hospitalized at Children's Psychiatric Hospital, University of Michigan Medical Center, Ann Arbor, Mich. The staff's conflicting perceptions of the children's reactions to the tragic event were strikingly evident. Torn between their own needs and those of the children, the staff was confused about the therapeutically appropriate means of exposing the children to the details of the assassination, the shooting of the accused assassin, and the funeral. Even experienced personnel, ordinarily intuitively responsive to the children's needs, were markedly uncertain about the handling of children at that time. Thus, the focus of investigation shifted from study of the reactions of the children to the exploration of conflicting staff perceptions and attitudes. This report of the staff's reactions is intended as a limited contribution to the accumulation of knowledge[1-5] concerning the capacities, perceptions, and behavior of interested adults dealing with bereaved children.

Method

Two types of observational data were studied. The first was the routine written reports of psychotherapists, nurses, child-care workers, teachers, occupational therapists, and recreational therapists. These were recorded at the time as a regular part of hospital procedure, and thus were in no way influenced by the present study. The second type of data was gathered retrospectively in the form of written material and group discussion, with staff representing various disciplines. These data were focused on the children's reactions and the patient-staff interaction, and were collected after this study was undertaken.

Observations

Staff Conceptions of How Children Should React.—There was considerable disagreement between staff members over what the children's appropriate response should be. Typically, staff members perceive and react to the children in a highly differentiated and understanding manner. However, in this instance their covert and, at times, overt expectations seemed to call for a uniform and "adult-like" reaction of soberness, if not downright grief. Indeed, the staff responded to children's jocular behavior and lack of reverence with moral indignation. A striking example was provided by a 12-year-old boy with ulcerative colitis who laughed when the bugler hit a wrong note while playing taps at the late President's funeral. Understandably, the staff's immediate reaction was one of distaste; but subsequently, over the course of the next two months, there appeared to be increasing difficulty in the interaction between this boy and ward staff. It should be noted that this connection had not been recognized until it was brought up in one of our retrospective meetings. On another occasion, the staff became indignant when some of the youngsters protested and expressed resentment about a party being cancelled on the evening of the President's assassination. It seemed as though the proper adult mourning attitude was expected of the children, regardless of their developmental stages or degree and kind of pathology.

Management of Children's Reactions.— There was uncertainty among staff members about how to respond to the children's reactions. In some instances, children's grief reactions appeared to be avoided by the staff. Several recorded observations noted that children failed to comment about the death, and staff members presumed the children were not reacting to it, despite noting a distinct behavioral change. For instance, an aggressive borderline psychotic 13-year-old girl, who suffered periods of depression, slept a great deal on the day of the President's assassination. This had been her usual behavior when depressed in the past. She mentioned dreaming about being killed, but reportedly "dropped the subject." Apparently the depressive reaction in this girl was either consciously or unconsciously ignored. Some of the staff seemed to focus on verbal reactions and responded to misbehavior with immediate firm controls. Other staff members perceived misbehavior as a means of mastering anxiety and, therefore, considered such behavior helpful. Also, assassination games, such as shooting or being shot, were tolerated—as if such identifications and repetitions were means of constructively mastering anxiety.

Degree of Exposure to the Details of the Tragedy.— In keeping with Children's Psychiatric Hospital's typical mode of individualizing each child's treatment, there were no general administrative directions as to how much the children should be exposed to details of the tragedy. Each ward was free to handle their patient's reactions individually. This resulted in a remarkable lack of agreement among ward staff about the proper amount of exposure for the children to the details of President Kennedy's assassination. Some staff members were convinced that television provided a vehicle for working through grief reactions to President

Kennedy's death; others disagreed, and were concerned about how to allow the children to watch "history in the making" while staying within the limits of what would not be emotionally harmful. As might be expected, these two opposing attitudes led to conflict and confusion about when and how long the children should watch the continuous television coverage of the events. Frequently, attempts were made to divert the children's attention from the repetitious broadcast. At times this seemed to be in response to the children's request; yet at other times, the children were frankly disinterested in diversions, and angry when denied the right to watch television.

In our intramural school, some of the teachers attempted to cover the subject of the President's assassination as a structured formal learning experience in the current events part of the class on the day following the funeral. Other teachers, however, assiduously avoided the subject; some despite the fact that the discussion of current events was scheduled for that day.

The Ability of Grieving Adults to Observe Objectively.—Retrospectively, there appeared to be numerous distortions in the staff's perceptions of children's reactions, apparently as consequences of the participant observers' own grief. For example, there was an isolated report claiming that an autistic 9-year-old girl demonstrated "an appropriate affect" in response to the assassination, contradicting several other reports describing no change in her usual bizarre behavior.

In another instance, during one of the rettrospective discussions, a nurse was unable to remember the presence of a particularly omnipotent, bizarre boy with whom she generally worked closely. In fact, she doubted that he had been admitted to the hospital by the time of the assassination. She felt that if he had been admitted, he must have gone home early that weekend. In contradiction to her conviction, there were many notes describing his usual bizarre behavior during the entire weekend.

Often it was impossible to decide whether a given instance represented misperception on the part of the staff, adaptation by the children to the behavior of bereaved adults, or manifest mourning on the part of the children.

Thus, the ward for the youngest and generally most regressed children reported an amazing unanimity of "mature" behavior and response. Far less fighting and bizarre behavior than usual was reported that week; the staff perceived this as expressive of consideration by the children for the adults' feelings. The accuracy of this surprising observation and the validity of the motivational explanation cannot be ascertained, and both shall have to remain open to question. If, however, we assume the observation is undistorted, there remains doubt as to whether the children's unusual behavior was a reaction to the tragic events, imitation of the adults, or adaptation to the emotional unavailability, and perhaps irritability, of the staff. Such difficulties in obtaining accurate behavioral observations, much less valid interpretations, was particularly evident in assessing the retrospective data.

The Effect of Adult Grief on Children's Reactions.—There were some instances in which it was clear that the child was responding not only to the President's assassination, but also to the reaction of the bereaved adults. For example, a 10-year-old boy with severe behavior problems watched adults carefully for cues in how to react, and tended to mirror what he observed. In the hospital's intramural school, there was a marked similarity between the staff's reaction and the children's reported reactions. The teachers tended to describe similar reactions from all their students, seeing them as a group rather than in terms of individual differences. It was difficult to avoid the feeling that these reports depended far more upon the observer than on the children observed.

Comment

Study of the observations and the reactions of children made by clinical child-care workers during a period of mass-mourning[6,7] demonstrated a striking degree of estrangement from the children, in marked contrast to the empathic relationship these same adults generally enjoyed with their charges. Furthermore, it should be noted that the observers were experienced in giving written and verbal reports about these children. At other times, and in relation to other issues, this was invariably accomplished without evidence of the massive misperceptions and distortions cited above.

Concurrently it was clear that the therapeutic staff were vague about children's concepts of death.[8-13] There was much uncertainty and disagreement on what children knew about death, how much information and emotional impact they could tolerate, what they should be exposed to, and in what fashion. Underlying some of the manifest attitudes appeared to be an assumption that children are incapable of possessing a reasonable concept of death. Paradoxically, this was often in juxtaposition with the expectation of an adult-like reaction from the children. At times, this was expressed in a tendency to dictate moralistically about how the children should behave and "properly grieve." Children who did not conform to this stereotype tended to be blamed, overtly or covertly, for alleged shortcomings. Stated briefly: "children don't know about death; yet they should mourn as adults do." This is remindful of Durkheim's[14] assertion that mourning is more than an expression of individual feelings, and also reflects a duty imposed by a group that forces one to weep.

There were surprisingly many instances in which otherwise sensitive and intuitive people thought the children were unaffected by the tragic events, despite their own observations of unequivocal behavioral shifts. One cannot help but wonder how much this reflects the ubiquitous fear of death[15] that results in a widespread denial of death's inevitability and finality—in essence, a societal evasion of the entire issue of death. Assisted by technological progress and urbanization, American culture seems involved in a conspiracy to remove death from conscious awareness. Bereavement has become an individual matter, with an attendant deritualization of mourning.[16-18] As institutional patterns diminish the bereaved are left increasingly to fend for themselves, with concomitant growth of uncertainty. Such an avoidant attitude on the part of our staff was in evidence; for example, in the failure of the administrative staff to give direction, and in the presence of the emotion-denying "history in the making" viewpoint.

It should be emphasized, however, that our society has never had much in the way of identifiable guidelines to follow in dealing with children's confrontations with death. Although the tendency of children to equate death with a long journey is no longer encouraged as much as in the past, by adults "protectively" telling children that a recently deceased relative has taken a long trip, we lack a ritualized prescription of what to tell children, what to do with them, what to have them do, etc. Anthropological reports occasionally mention the role of the "children of the deceased" in the death rituals of other cultures, but indications as to the age of the participating offspring are rarely found.

Mandelbaum[18] mentions the well-defined special ceremonial roles for the children of the recently deceased in the Kota (India) "dry funeral," a communal event celebrated every year or two. Stewart[19] describes that, following death until the funeral feast, the children of a deceased Negrito (Phillipines) are expected to dream repeatedly of their parent and be willing to do whatever request is made in the dream. In neither of these reports, however, are there any hints as to how young the "children" are. Fortes,[20] on the other hand, describes the ritual of headshaving practiced by children, as young as 10 years, of deceased Tallensi (Africa). Furthermore, the youngest grandchildren of the deceased Tallensi are assigned a ritualized role in the funeral.

Does our staff's display of confusion relate also to some aspects of the controversies[21-28] about the incidence and duration of children's manifest depressive reactions stimulated by object loss, as well as their capacity to work through the mourning process adequately? Certainly, our experiences suggest that one should question the validity of accepting the descriptions of children's bereavement reactions given by mourning adults. In our data it was impossible to distinguish between adult misperceptions and confusions, the children's reaction to the tragedy, and the children's reaction to the changes in the adults.

When a young parent dies, the children are often immediately shunted off to the homes, of relatives or friends. This is frequently accomplished without the active participation of the surviving parent, whose profound grief and shock may render him incapable of providing even the most basic and minimal care for his children. Furthermore, the helpful relatives and friends who bring the children to their homes typically leave them in the care of older cousins or sitters as they return to the surviving parent, whose manifest need for help is often so much more obvious than the children's. Thus, retrospective investigators[29] may be forced to rely on reports from people whose perceptive apparatus were blurred by overwhelming emotion. Clearly, there is a great need for continuing "objective" observations, despite the fact that objectivity is impossible for a feeling person to attain when dealing with a small child whose parent has just died.

Summary

Following the assassination of President Kennedy, the staff of Children's Psychiatric Hospital, torn between their own grief and the needs of the children, manifested a significantly atypical amount of confusion and

173

insensitivity in their handling of the children. This highlighted the lack of societal guidelines or rituals for dealing with children's confrontations with death in our culture. Furthermore, the staff's descriptions of the children's reactions were so riddled with disagreements and distortions that one cannot help but raise questions about the validity of accounts of children's bereavement reactions given by mourning adults—just such accounts as figure prominently in our growing literature on childhood bereavement.

Annette McDaniels, Sue Packard, Iveta Priede, Nadine Pringle, Mary Resnick, and Rita Robbins assisted in collecting and organizing the data.

References

1. Becker, D., and Margolin, F.: Parental Attitudes Towards the Young Child's Adaptation to the Crisis of Loss, read before the 43rd annual meeting of the American Orthopsychiatric Association, San Francisco, April 1966.

2. Mahler, M.: Helping Children to Accept Death, *Child Study* 27(4):98-99, 119-120 (Fall) 1950.

3. Mohr, G.: *When Children Face Crises*, Chicago: Science Research Associates, 1952.

4. Sherrill, L.J., and Sherrill, H.H.: Interpreting Death to Children, *Int J Religious Educ* 27:4-6 (Oct) 1951.

5. Wolf, A.W.M.: *Helping Your Child to Understand Death*, New York: Child Study Association of America, 1958.

6. Volkart, B.: "Bereavement and Mental Health," in Leighton, A., et al (eds.): *Explorations in Social Psychiatry*, New York: Basic Books Inc., 1957.

7. Wolfenstein, M., and Kliman, G.: *Children's Reactions to the Death of the President,* New York: Doubleday Book Co., 1965.

8. Anthony, S.: *The Child's Discovery of Death,* New York: Harcourt, Brace, and World, 1940.

9. Bender, L.: *Aggression, Hostility, and Anxiety in Children,* Springfield, Ill: Charles C Thomas Publishers, 1913.

10. Fast, I., and Cain, A.C.: Children's Distorted Concepts of Death, read before the 40th annual meeting of the American Orthopsychiatric Association, Washington, March 1963.

11. Nagy, M.: "The Child's View of Death," in Feifel, H. (ed.): *The Meaning of Death,* New York: McGraw-Hill Book Co., Inc., 1959.

12. Pieper, W.S.: How Children Conceive of Death, read before the Area IV divisional meeting of the American Psychiatric Association, St. Louis, October 1965.

13. Schilder, P., and Wechsler, D.: The Attitudes of Children Toward Death, *J Genet Psychol* **45**:406-451, 1934.

14. Durkheim, E.: *The Elementary Forms of the Religious Life,* London: George Allen & Unwin Ltd., 1915.

15. Wahl, C.W.: "The Fear of Death," in Feifel, H. (ed.): *The Meaning of Death,* New York: McGraw-Hill Book Co., Inc., 1959.

16. Krupp, G.R.: The Bereavement Reaction: A Special Case of Separation Anxiety—Sociocultural Considerations, *Psychoanal Stud Soc* **2**:42-74, 1962.

17. Krupp, G.R., and Kligfield, B.: The Bereavement Reaction: A Crosscultural Evaluation, *J Religion Health* **1**:223-246, 1946.

18. Mandelbaum, D.G.: "Social Uses of Funeral Rites," in Feifel, H. (ed.): *The Meaning of Death,* New York: McGraw-Hill Book Co., Inc., 1959.

19. Stewart, K.: *Pygmies and Dream Giants,* New York: W.W. Norton & Co., 1954.

20. Fortes, M.: *The Web of Kinship Among the Tallensi,* London: Oxford University Press, 1944.

21. Bowlby, J.: Grief and Mourning in Infancy and Early Childhood, *Psychoanal Stud Child* **15**:9-52, 1960.

22. Deutsch, H.: Absence of Grief, *Psychoanal Quart* **6**:12-22, 1937.

23. Freud, A., and Burlingham, D.: *Infants Without Families,* New York: International Universities Press, 1944.

24. Freud, A.: Discussion of Bowlby, *Psychoanal Stud Child* **15**:53-62, 1960.

25. Magler, M.: On Sadness and Grief in Infancy and Childhood, *Psychoanal Stud Child* **16**:332-351, 1961.

26. Rochlin, G.: The Loss Complex, *J Amer Psychoanal Assoc* **7**:299-315, 1959.

27. Schur, M.: Discussion of Bowlby, *Psychoanal Stud Child* **15**:53-84, 1960.

175

28. Spitz, R.: Discussion of Bowlby, *Psychoanal Stud Child* **15:**85-94, 1960.

29. Cain, A.; Fast, I.; and Erikson, M.E.: Children's Disturbed Reactions to the Death of a Sibling, *Amer J Orthopsychiat* **34:**741-752, 1964.

AUTHOR INDEX

Alltop, Lacoe B., 133

Birtchnell, John, 11, 31, 56,
   71, 91, 112
Bratfos, Ole, 140
Buffaloe, W.J., 133

Davenport, Charles W., 166

Harrison, Saul I., 166

Jacobson, Gary, 149

McDermott, Jr., John F., 166

Ryder, Robert G., 149

Wilson, Ian C., 133

KEY-WORD TITLE INDEX

Bereavement,
   Children's Reaction to, 166
   Parental, in Childhood, 133

Childhood, Parental Deprivation in, 140

Early Parent Death,
   Consequences of, 31
   Interrelationship between
     Social Class, Mental Ill-
     ness, and, 91
   Mental Illness and, 91

Psychiatric Diagnosis and,
   11
Relation to Size and Constitution of Sibship, 112

Marriage Relationship, Parental
   Loss and Some Characteris-
   tics of the Early, 149
M.M.P.I., Profiles in a
   Depressed Population, 133

Recent Parent Death, Mental
   Illness and, 71

177